Golf Rules & Etiquette For Dummies

On the Course Do's and Don'ts

Do:

- Play at a reasonable pace.
- Repair ball marks, replace divots, and rake bunkers.
- Pay attention to the rules as they are laid out and administered by the R&A and the USGA.
- Have the player who is farthest away from the pin hit first on each shot.
- Let the winner of the previous hole tee off first at the next tee.
- Take a caddie whenever possible.
- Turn in every score for handicap purposes.
- Respect the rules and regulations of the course you are playing.

Don't:

- Move or talk while someone in your group is hitting the ball (or about to hit).
- Ask your opponent what club he hit.
- Walk across the line of another player's putt on the green.
- Hit your shots until the group in front of you is well out of range.
- Ever play when lightning is in the area.
- Be like Rodney Dangerfield in *Caddyshack*. (Whenever you go out to play, remember that understated is best.)
- Hold up other players.

Do's and Don'ts for Golf Spectators

Do:

- Be quiet when play is going on.
- Keep your movements to a minimum when players are about to hit.
- Wait for all players to putt out before leaving the green area for the next tee.
- Follow the etiquette guidelines set down by the club and association hosting the event.
- Cheer a good shot, but only in an appropriate and moderate fashion.
- Wear sneakers or spikeless golf shoes on the course, to help with wear and tear.

Don't:

- Run around a golf course while a tournament is being played.
- Talk on a cell phone.
- Take pictures during competition rounds. Always check with tournament organizers to see what the rules are.
- Ask for autographs from golfers who are still out on the course playing.
- Holler "You da man!" after a player has hit a shot.
- Applaud or otherwise ridicule a bad shot by one of the players.

For Dummies™*: Bestselling Book Series for Beginners*

Golf Rules & Etiquette For Dummies®

Business Outing Do's and Don'ts

Do:

- ✔ Respect the course you are playing and leave it in as good shape as you found it.
- ✔ Act like a guest and adhere to all rules and regulations of the venue.
- ✔ Buy something from the pro shop, as a gesture of support for the pro.
- ✔ Thank the staff and whomever else has taken care of you that day.
- ✔ Keep bad language and a fierce temper in check.
- ✔ Write a thank-you note to your host.

Don't:

- ✔ Use an out-of-date handicap, especially if yours is higher than it should be.
- ✔ Play slowly. Outing golf can take forever as it is, so do what you can to speed things along.
- ✔ Show up late.
- ✔ Drink too much.
- ✔ Keep playing if you are out of a hole.

How to Score Common Penalty Shots

Penalty	How to Score
Out-of-bounds	Stroke and distance; 2-stroke penalty.
Unplayable lies	1-stroke penalty. Drop the ball within two club lengths of the original spot, no nearer to the hole. Or drop the ball as far back as you want, as long as you keep the original unplayable lie point between you and the hole. You may also return to the spot from which you played your original shot if you prefer.
Water hazard (yellow stakes)	Play the ball as near as possible to the place from which the original shot was hit. Or drop a ball behind the water, as long as you keep the point at which the original ball crossed the edge of the water hazard directly between the hole and the spot on which the ball is dropped. There is no limit to how far behind the water hazard you can go with the ball.
Lateral water hazard (red stakes)	Use the preceding two rules for a regular water hazard (yellow stakes). Then drop a ball outside the lateral hazard within two club lengths of where the ball went in, but not nearer to the hole. Or keep a point on the opposite edge of the water hazard equidistant from the hole.

For Dummies™: Bestselling Book Series for Beginners

Praise for Golf Rules & Etiquette For Dummies

"I picked up my first golf club at age 10, and I also threw my first and last club at age 10. I will never forget that day when my father walked me off the course and told me that if he ever saw me throw another club, it would be the last round of golf I would ever play. I was fortunate in that I learned at an early age about the rules and etiquette of this great game. I also know that it is never too late to learn the subtleties that make up the traditions of golf, and that learning rules and etiquette can be fun. John Steinbreder delivers that in an easy-to-understand and humorous way. After all, this game was meant to be fun."

— Jack Nicklaus

"I have not only a passion for the game of golf, but also for the way it is played, and that means both rules and etiquette are very important to me. With his latest publication, John Steinbreder has written the book on both those two subjects and done so with equal doses of authority and humor. It is a must-read for anyone who plays golf, and fun to read as well."

— Jim Baugh, President, Wilson Sporting Goods

"As someone firmly ensconced within the numbers of high handicap golfers in the United States, I am uniquely qualified to state that John Steinbreder's *Golf Rules & Etiquette For Dummies* will be the definitive resource for his target audience."

— Ty M. Votaw, Commissioner, Ladies Professional Golf Association

"Steinbreder has done a great job at making the rules and etiquette of golf *fun!* Easy to read and very educational."

— Bob Ford, golf professional, Oakmont Country Club, Seminole Golf Club

"John's understanding of the ins and outs and ups and downs of the game of golf, as a player and a student, shine through in this book. Having played with him numerous times, the book is proof of the old saying 'Those who can do, those who can't teach.' It's a terrific book!"

— J.S. Berrien, president, *Forbes* magazine

Golf Rules
& Etiquette
FOR
DUMMIES®

Golf Rules & Etiquette FOR DUMMIES

by John Steinbreder

Hungry Minds™

HUNGRY MINDS, INC.

New York, NY ◆ Cleveland, OH ◆ Indianapolis, IN

Golf Rules & Etiquette For Dummies®

Published by
Hungry Minds, Inc.
An International Data Group Company
909 Third Avenue, 21st Floor
New York, NY 10022
www.hungryminds.com (Hungry Minds Web Site)
www.dummies.com (Dummies Web Site)

Library of Congress Control Number: 00-111127

ISBN: 0-7645-5333-X

Printed in the United States of America

10 9 8 7 6 5 4 3

1B/RT/QT/QR/IN

Distributed in the United States by Hungry Minds, Inc.

Distributed by CDG Books Canada Inc. for Canada; by Transworld Publishers Limited in the United Kingdom; by IDG Norge Books for Norway; by IDG Sweden Books for Sweden; by IDG Books Australia Publishing Corporation Pty. Ltd. for Australia and New Zealand; by TransQuest Publishers Pte Ltd. for Singapore, Malaysia, Thailand, Indonesia, and Hong Kong; by Gotop Information Inc. for Taiwan; by ICG Muse, Inc. for Japan; by Intersoft for South Africa; by Eyrolles for France; by International Thomson Publishing for Germany, Austria and Switzerland; by Distribuidora Cuspide for Argentina; by LR International for Brazil; by Galileo Libros for Chile; by Ediciones ZETA S.C.R. Ltda. for Peru; by WS Computer Publishing Corporation, Inc., for the Philippines; by Contemporanea de Ediciones for Venezuela; by Express Computer Distributors for the Caribbean and West Indies; by Micronesia Media Distributor, Inc. for Micronesia; by Chips Computadoras S.A. de C.V. for Mexico; by Editorial Norma de Panama S.A. for Panama; by American Bookshops for Finland.

For general information on Hungry Minds's books in the U.S., please call our Consumer Customer Service department at 800-762-2974. For reseller information, including discounts and premium sales, please call our Reseller Customer Service department at 800-434-3422.

For information on where to purchase Hungry Minds's books outside the U.S., please contact our International Sales department at 317-572-3993 or fax 317-572-4002.

For consumer information on foreign language translations, please contact our Customer Service department at 1-800-434-3422, fax 317-572-4002, or e-mail rights@idgbooks.com.

For information on licensing foreign or domestic rights, please phone +1-650-653-7098.

For sales inquiries and special prices for bulk quantities, please contact our Order Services department at 800-434-4322 or write to the address above.

For information on using Hungry Minds's books in the classroom or for ordering examination copies, please contact our Educational Sales department at 800-434-2086 or fax 317-572-4005.

For press review copies, author interviews, or other publicity information, please contact our Public Relations department at 650-653-7000 or fax 650-653-7500.

For authorization to photocopy items for corporate, personal, or educational use, please contact Copyright Clearance Center, 222 Rosewood Drive, Danvers, MA 01923, or fax 978-750-4470.

Hungry Minds™ is a trademark of Hungry Minds, Inc.

About the Author

John Steinbreder is a senior writer for *Golfweek* magazine and the author of six books. A former reporter for
Fortune magazine and writer/reporter for *Sports
Illustrated,* he has been honored by the Golf Writers
Association of America for his work and has had his
writing published in a number of top periodicals, including *The New York Times Magazine, Forbes FYI, Time, The
Wall Street Journal,* and *Sky.* He also served for a time as
a special contributor to ESPN Television and is now a
contributing editor to *Met Golfer, Sporting Classics,* and
Chief Executive magazines. An avid golfer who carries a 5
handicap (most of the time), Steinbreder lives in Easton,
Connecticut, with his 9-year-old daughter, Exa.

Dedication

For my father, Sandy Steinbreder, who introduced me to this great game of golf. And for my daughter, Exa, who is letting me do the same for her.

Author's Acknowledgments

There are, I have found, remarkable similarities between two things that occupy a great deal of my time these days — golf and writing. Both are often solitary pursuits, and it is almost impossible to be any good at them without lots of help. Caddies, for example, make sure their players survive all the ups and downs a round frequently brings. And friends, agents, editors, and sources assist writers in getting their work done well and on schedule, and in keeping their sanity throughout the process. So it is not surprising that in writing a book about golf, I found that I needed — and received — lots of help. And it is easy for me to say without the slightest bit of hyperbole that I could not have completed this opus without it.

It was Mark Reiter of the International Management Group and Stacy Collins of Hungry Minds who brought me into this project and helped see it through. Mark is a terrific agent who is always looking for ways to make me more solvent, and I appreciate his efforts. As for Stacy, she represents everything a writer wants in a publisher, and I am grateful for her friendship, enthusiasm, hard work, and choice of restaurants in Chicago. I also admire the deft way with which she cracks the whip; I guess all writers need to get roughed up on occasion.

In addition, I am thankful for the fine editing skills — and saintly patience — of my editor, Elizabeth Kuball, as well as the aid of Stacy Klein and Tracy Boggier of Hungry Minds. Then, of course, there is Jack Druga, a PGA professional who served as Technical Editor. Jack is not only a keen student of the game and a valuable source but also a good friend and a topflight player and teacher. He selflessly completed his work in the midst of some terribly trying personal times.

I spoke with dozens of sources during the writing of this book, and there are several I am deeply indebted to, including Mark McCormack, who is always available to help out; Alastair Johnston, another valuable and accessible contact; Jack Nicklaus, the paragon of the gentleman golfer; Jeff Hall and the people at the United States Golf Association for all their assistance and counsel; Hootie Johnson and Glenn Greenspan from Augusta National; Willie Nelson for his time and, of course, his music; Larry Lambrecht for his photographs; Herky Williams, Rich Katz, Vinnie Giles, Scott Tolley, Terry McSweeney, Leslie King, and Chris Millard for running interference; Tom Graham for his friendship, insight, and sportsmanship; Brian Hewitt, who provided good information from the tours he covers so well; Bob Ford, who never fails to return a phone call; Mike Downey, for all he taught me over the years; Joe Cantwell, for his words of wisdom; Millie Foote, for never sugarcoating it; and Ken Baron, for his articles on business golf. I would also like to thank Sean McManus, Jim Baugh, Billy Casper, and Ty Votaw for their endorsements; Jeff Bernstein, for his sharp pencil; Renee for her phone calls and friendship (even though she did walk away); and those roguish men of goat, Duncan Christy, Tim Harper, and John McLaughlin, for their incomparable inspiration.

Over the past 20 years, I have been fortunate to make a nice living as a writer, and I am especially pleased that golf has become the primary focus of my work. It is a great sport, and I am very fond of the friendships and business associations I have made through the game. Among the relationships I value most dearly are those I have established with the folks who run *Golfweek.* I owe a tremendous debt of gratitude to Dave Seanor, Jim Nugent, Dale Gardner, Gene Yasuda, Jeff Babineau, Alayna Gaines, and Bradley Klein for all they do to make my job there fun and stimulating. I must also acknowledge those who print — and pay for — my work elsewhere, especially Il Duce at *Sky Magazine,* Patrick Cooke and Christopher Buckley at *Forbes FYI,* Robin McMillan at *Met Golfer,* and J.P. Donlan at *Chief Executive.* And I would be remiss if I did not express my appreciation to some of the people who have educated me about the golf business over the past couple of years and always answered my sometimes stupid questions, among them Wally Uihlein, George Sine, Luke Reese, Ely Callaway, Larry Dorman, Barney Adams, Joe Gomes, Ed Abrain, Jeff Sernick, Jackie Beck, Eddie Binder, and Casey Alexander.

On a personal note, golf has been an important part of my life for much of my 44 years, and few things give me as much pleasure as a weekend morning round with my friends. There is no one I enjoy playing with as much as Nat Foote, and I am glad we have had so many great times together on the links. There are others who have made my golf games memorable, including John Akers, Peter Dunn, Bob Bruder, Jim Berrien, Whit Foote, Bobby Bigonette, Henry and Cammie Bertram, Stephen Murray, Tom Kreitler, David Rosow, Dick McConn, Tim Kennedy, Peter Foote, Richie Tilghman, Ocie Adams, Tom Crolius, David Owen, Jerry Tarde, Eric Purcell, Craig Atkinson, George Rippey, Jeff Earls, John Davidson, Fran Johnson, Pat Byrne, Bill Gray, Jack and Jane Welch, and Peter Britton. Thanks, everyone; let's play golf all the time!

Alas, some of those I am closest to rarely make it out to the course. But that does not diminish the positive ways they impact my life. So here's to my mother, Cynthia, now 70 years young and still cheering me on; my sisters Sissy, Gillett, and Sarah for the champagne we shared the night I finished this book; and my very own Dixie Chick, who spreads dittos all around.

Finally, I must pay special tribute to my 9-year-old daughter, Exa, for her love, warmth, and understanding; for her cheerful and caring disposition; for those breakfasts she cooks me (even though it takes days to clean the pans afterward); for understanding why I drop her off at Granny's some weekend mornings so I can get my rounds in; and for always asking first thing when I return, "Daddy, how was the sweet swing?" Never as sweet as it is to see her, I always say. And for that, I am eternally grateful.

Publisher's Acknowledgments

We're proud of this book; please send us your comments through our Hungry Minds Online Registration Form located at www.dummies.com.

Some of the people who helped bring this book to market include the following:

Acquisitions, Editorial, and Media Development

Project Editor: Elizabeth Netedu Kuball

Acquisitions Editor: Stacy S. Collins

Acquisitions Coordinator: Stacy Klein

Technical Editor: Jack Druga

Editorial Manager: Jennifer Ehrlich

Editorial Assistant: Carol Strickland

Cover Photos: © FPG International/ Jim Cummins

Production

Project Coordinator: Dale White

Layout and Graphics: Amy Adrian, Kelly Hardesty, Jeremey Unger

Special Art: Precision Graphics

Proofreaders: Sally Barton, Susan Moritz, Angel Perez, York Production Services, Inc.

Indexer: York Production Services, Inc.

General and Administrative

Hungry Minds, Inc.: John Kilcullen, CEO; Bill Barry, President and COO; John Ball, Executive VP, Operations & Administration; John Harris, CFO

Hungry Minds Consumer Reference Group

    Business: Kathleen A. Welton, Vice President and Publisher; Kevin Thornton, Acquisitions Manager

    Cooking/Gardening: Jennifer Feldman, Associate Vice President and Publisher

    Education/Reference: Diane Graves Steele, Vice President and Publisher; Greg Tubach, Publishing Director

    Lifestyles: Kathleen Nebenhaus, Vice President and Publisher; Tracy Boggier, Managing Editor

    Pets: Dominique De Vito, Associate Vice President and Publisher; Tracy Boggier, Managing Editor

    Travel: Michael Spring, Vice President and Publisher; Suzanne Jannetta, Editorial Director; Brice Gosnell, Managing Editor

Hungry Minds Consumer Editorial Services: Kathleen Nebenhaus, Vice President and Publisher; Kristin A. Cocks, Editorial Director; Cindy Kitchel, Editorial Director

Hungry Minds Consumer Production: Debbie Stailey, Production Director

◆

The publisher would like to give special thanks to Patrick J. McGovern, without whom this book would not have been possible.

◆

Contents at a Glance

Introduction 1

Part I: You've Got to Play by the Rules 7
Chapter 1: We Didn't Make the Rules 9
Chapter 2: It's Not Just a Game (Why Golfers Are So
Devoted to Golf).. 25
Chapter 3: The Rules (And I'm Not Talking about Dating)................... 33

Part II: The Unwritten Rules: How to Handle Yourself
on (And off) the Course 53
Chapter 4: Universal Truths and Other Rules to Live By...................... 55
Chapter 5: This Isn't Caddyshack: Playing on Public
and Private Courses 73
Chapter 6: Driving Ranges, Putting Greens, and Other Practice
Facilities.. 79
Chapter 7: Taking Care of Business 87

Part III: Even More Rules . . . For Players
and Spectators 99
Chapter 8: The Do's and Don'ts of Golf Outings................................ 101
Chapter 9: Keeping Your Cool on the Course: Fan Etiquette.............. 107

Part IV: The Part of Tens 117
Chapter 10: The Ten Most Devastating Penalties 119
Chapter 11: The Ten Best Games and Bets to Make in Golf................ 125
Chapter 12: Ten Things You Can Learn about Golf Rules
and Etiquette from the Movies.. 133

Part V: Appendixes 139
Appendix A 141
Appendix B 147

Index.. 159
Book Registration Information .... Back of Book

Cartoons at a Glance

By Rich Tennant

page 53

page 139

page 99

page 7

page 117

Cartoon Information:
Fax: 978-546-7747
E-Mail: richtennant@the5thwave.com
World Wide Web: www.the5thwave.com

Table of Contents

Introduction **1**

    About This Book 1
    Foolish Assumptions 2
    Why You Need This Book...2
    How This Book Is Organized 4
        Part I: You've Got to Play by the Rules 4
        Part II: The Unwritten Rules: How to Handle Yourself
          on (And off) the Course 4
        Part III: Even More Rules . . . For Players and Spectators 5
        Part IV: The Part of Tens...5
        Part V: Appendixes 5
    Icons Used in This Book...5
    Where to Go from Here 6

Part 1: You've Got to Play by the Rules.........................7

    Chapter 1: We Didn't Make the Rules 9

        Taking a Brief Historical Glance at the Rules of Golf......................9
        Figuring Out How, When, and Why the Rules Were Formed 11
        Recognizing the People and Organizations Who Developed
          and Enforced the Rules 13
          The R&A...13
          The USGA...15
        Understanding the Importance of Knowing and Following
          the Rules...16
        Taking a Look at the Best and Worst of the Rules 18
          The five best rules in golf 18
          The five dumbest rules in golf 19
          The most controversial rule in golf today......................20

    Chapter 2: It's Not Just a Game (Why Golfers Are So
    Devoted to Golf)...25

        Why Golf Is Different from Other Sports....................................26
        The Devotion Players Have for the Rules That Govern Golf 28
        A Plea for Common Sense...30
        A Plea for TV Viewers to Put Down the Phone.............................31

    Chapter 3: The Rules (And I'm Not Talking about Dating)....33

        Fifteen of the Most Important Rules in Golf 34
          Rule 1-1: The Game — General......................................34
          Rule 2-1: The Match — Winner of Hole; Reckoning
            of Holes 34
          Rules 3-1 and 3-2: Stroke play......................................34
          Rule 4-4: Clubs — Maximum of 14 Clubs 35

Rule 5-3: The Ball — Ball Unfit for Play 35
Rules 7-1 and 7-2: Practice 36
Rules 8-1 and 8-2: Advice; Indicating Line of Play 37
Rule 13-1: Ball Played as It Lies 38
Rule 16-1 and 16-2: The Putting Green 38
Rule 17-1, 17-3: The Flagstick 41
Rule 23: Loose Impediments 41
Rules 24-1 and 24-2: Obstructions, Movable
      and Immovable 42
Rule 26-1: Water Hazards — Ball in Water Hazard 44
Rules 27-1 and 27-2: Ball Lost or Out of Bounds;
      Provisional Ball 45
Rule 28: Ball Unplayable 47
How the Rules Have Been Interpreted 48
Do it once more, with feeling 49
I am a rock 49
Say again 50
"What a stupid I am!" 50

Part II: The Unwritten Rules: How to Handle Yourself on (And off) the Course 53

Chapter 4: Universal Truths and Other Rules to Live By 55

Golf Etiquette 101: The Basics 56
Playing in Tournaments 60
Working with the Handicap System 64
Playing with Caddies 66
Tipping Gracefully 71

Chapter 5: This Isn't Caddyshack: Playing on Public and Private Courses 73

Knowing the Municipal Course Basics 73
Playing at a High-End "Country-Club-for-a- Day" Course 75
Teeing It Up at a Private Club 75

Chapter 6: Driving Ranges, Putting Greens, and Other Practice Facilities 79

Driving Ranges 79
Watch where you're aiming 80
Leave the range balls on the range 80
Pay for your range balls 80
Hit your balls between the ropes 81
Stay off the range when it's open 82
Putting Greens 82
Treat the putting green as you would any green
      on the course 83
Don't use more than a couple balls when you're
      practicing 83
Pay attention to which pin you're putting at 83

Don't assume chipping around the putting green
is allowed 83
Use practice greens as a way to introduce the game
to your kids..84
Other Practice Facilities...84

Chapter 7: Taking Care of Business...............................87

Playing Golf with Your Clients...87
Make sure your clients enjoy the game
before inviting them 88
Inform your partners of the dress code and other rules....88
Compliment your clients on their game 88
Help your clients look for lost balls 89
Don't talk business every minute.......................................89
Don't be a teacher 89
Walk whenever possible 91
Look the other way if your client breaks a rule
here or there..91
Playing Golf with Your Boss...92
Understanding the Do's and Don'ts of Some Key Issues
in the Game of Golf 94
Winning 94
Betting...94
Telling jokes..95
Drinking...95
Cell phones 97

Part III: Even More Rules . . . For Players
and Spectators...99

Chapter 8: The Do's and Don'ts of Golf Outings..................101

Business-Related Golf Outings 101
Charity Golf Outings 103
Pro-Am Tournaments...104

Chapter 9: Keeping Your Cool on the Course:
Fan Etiquette...107

Attending Golf Tournaments 107
Desperately Seeking Autographs 111

Part IV: The Part of Tens 117

Chapter 10: The Ten Most Devastating Penalties.................119

Bad Hands...120
Bad Throw 120
Bad Drop 120
Bad Question 121
Bad Agreement...121
Bad Club...121
Bad Decision...122

Bad Practice..122
Bad Swing..122
Bad Luck...123
Bad Idea...123

**Chapter 11: The Ten Best Games and Bets to Make
in Golf 125**

Nassau..127
Skins..128
Wolf..128
Points...129
Dollar a Yard 129
Pink Lady...129
Junk or Side Cheese...129
Playing with the Pro 130
Hog Press 130
The Big Hawaiian 130

**Chapter 12: Ten Things You Can Learn about Golf Rules
and Etiquette from the Movies...................................133**

When You Hit into the Water, Drop a New Ball Where the First
One Entered the Hazard 133
Never Land a Helicopter While Players Are Teeing Off..............134
Avoid Thunderstorms 134
Watch Where You Hit Your Ball..134
Keep Your Eye on Your Ball — and Your Caddy 134
Know Where to Drop 135
Don't Take Advice from Anyone Other Than Your Caddy..........135
Keep It Moving 136
Be Silent When Other Golfers Are Hitting the Ball 136
Always Pay What You Owe 136

Part V: Appendixes *139*

Appendix A **141**

Appendix B **147**

Web Sites..147
Golf Associations 149

Index *159*

Book Registration Information....................*Back of Book*

Introduction

· ·

Welcome to *Golf Rules & Etiquette For Dummies,* which makes sense of those two very important parts of the game. No, I do not show you how to swing a 6-iron or hit a flop wedge. Nor do I list my favorite golf courses and give you tips on how to watch tournaments on television. That's what Gary McCord does in the best-selling *Golf For Dummies,* 2nd Edition, and there is no reason for me to duplicate his good work. Instead, I am here to tell you about those all-important rules that govern the wonderful game of golf and describe the basic etiquette for playing — and watching — the sport.

About This Book

Dozens of books have been written about the rules of golf, including the bible on the subject, known appropriately as *The Official Rules of Golf* and published by the United States Golf Association, which is one of the governing bodies of the game. Other books, like *Golf For Dummies,* touch on issues of etiquette as well. But as far as I know, this is the only book that covers both subjects with equal emphasis and authority — and does so with comparable doses of knowledge, humor, and fun.

Are you allowed to tee your ball up in the rough if your drive fades off to the right of the fairway? May you fix a spike mark on a green that stands between your ball and the cup? Is it legal to ask your opponent what club he or she has just hit? And what happens if you write down the wrong score on your scorecard while playing a tournament and don't notice the mistake until after you have signed it?

If you want a poster boy for bad behavior on the golf course, cue up *Caddyshack* on your VCR and watch Rodney Dangerfield as he terrorizes the "snobatorium" of Bushwood Country Club. No, it is not a good idea to drive your Rolls Royce onto the 1st tee. And hollering bets at members when you are just a guest is definitely taboo. So is insulting the wife of a member with lines like, "The last time I saw a mouth like that, it had a hook in it." And never, ever turn on the cassette player in your bag when another member of your foursome is about to swing.

But etiquette isn't as simple as it may sound. For example, did you know that you shouldn't bring a cell phone onto a golf course (unless you are a doctor on call or an expectant father who may need to make a run to the hospital before the turn). Talking on a cell phone while you're on the golf course is disturbing to everyone in your group, is boorish and rude, and in the vast majority of cases is absolutely unnecessary. You also shouldn't talk while someone is swinging, and you should always replace your divots and fix your ball marks. And don't ever scream at, berate, or abuse a caddie — or anyone else who is working at the course you are playing.

In some European countries, people cannot play golf unless they have earned a sort of certificate from the local pro that attests to the fact that they not only know how to swing a golf club but also have a basic understanding of the rules and etiquette of the game. It's sort of like a driver's license for golfers. We have no such system in the United States, and some people view that as a near-tragedy, especially with all the new players coming into the game. But now we have *Golf Rules & Etiquette For Dummies,* which makes the sport easier to play and understand.

Foolish Assumptions

When it comes to you, the reader of this book, I make very few assumptions other than that you have some level of interest in the game of golf. This book is for golfers of all backgrounds and abilities, from the 9-year-old girl taking her first lesson to the 84-year-old duffer who tees it up at his local course every weekend. Whether you're a high-rolling country clubber or you play regular $10 rounds at your neighborhood muni track, you'll find lots of useful information in these pages. High school players will garner better knowledge of the game, and businessmen and -women who find that golf is now a much bigger part of their work will be able to make the transition from the boardroom to the putting green with ease. Even competitive amateur players and professionals can pick up some helpful tips in these pages, because the rules and etiquette of the game of golf can be complicated — and even the most experienced players don't know it all.

Why You Need This Book

All sports have their own sets of tried and true rules. They also have different nuances as well as generally accepted principles that dictate behavior both on and off the actual field of play.

All sports have these rules, but none are guided by quite as many — or are inclined to take them quite as seriously — as golf. Consider, for example, the 34 rules that govern the game. They are an intricate and often complicated compendium of dos and don'ts that have been developed and promoted over the past couple of centuries by rather high-minded and tradition-steeped organizations located on both sides of the Atlantic. In addition, numerous unwritten axioms have been handed down from generation to generation and are applied to all golfers when they play the game, whether good or bad, male or female, young or old. They are, in essence, a code of behavior that every person who tees up a Titleist is expected to abide by.

In many ways, those two things reflect a lot of what golf really is: a game of rules and etiquette. To be sure, golf is also about smoothing approach shots, powering drives, and draining putts. But rules and etiquette are in many ways its soul and guts, and the sport would not be what it is without those rules and the universal way players all over the world follow them.

So if you really want to enjoy the game of golf, you need this book. When you have a question about the rules, or as you head out the door to watch a tournament, you'll happily turn to this book because nothing else provides such a complete explanation of the rules of the game without putting you to sleep. (And believe me, as important as the USGA's rules publication may be, it can only be read successfully after several double espressos.)

Golf Rules & Etiquette For Dummies describes how and when the rules of golf were made and why they are followed so closely. Plus, I cover most of the unwritten rules as they relate to course behavior and etiquette, whether you are playing a public course, a high-end daily-fee layout, or hobnobbing with the rich and famous at some big-time country club. Read it, and you will get the information you need to play business golf (whether with your boss or your clients) or compete in tournaments and charity outings. You'll find tips on tipping as well as thoughts on betting, drinking, and appropriate golf attire. Whether you've been playing for years or are just figuring out which end of the putter to hold, this book has plenty of useful information for you. (And it won't be a bad birthday gift for your friends down at the office either.)

So, who am I to be giving you all this advice (and making you pay for it, too)? To start with, I am a senior writer for *Golfweek* magazine, a leading publication based in Orlando, Florida, and I have been covering the game for several years. I am also a contributing editor to *Met Golfer* magazine, a regional publication for the metropolitan New York area, and I also wrote about golf on occasion when I worked on the staff of *Sports Illustrated.* In addition, I have produced five books over the past decade, one of which was about golf's grandest tournament, the U.S. Open, and have been recognized for my work by the Golf Writers Association of America.

But I am more than some guy in baggy pants and a Hawaiian shirt who hangs out in the press room at major tournaments exchanging stories with my fellow journalists as I munch on donuts and drink black coffee. I also play the game, and at the moment carry a 5 handicap. I compete in a fair amount of tournaments and battle through lots of weekend Nassau (just one of many betting games I discuss in this book). I belong to a country club in my home state of Connecticut and served for a while there as chairman of the golf committee. (In essence, I was one of the people who ran the golf program, and when I wasn't trying to break 80, I was often asked to interpret rules during tournaments or chastise deviant members for various violations of etiquette. And believe me, there were plenty.) In addition, I have played on all types of courses and visited all kinds of facilities, from some of the most ragged public tracks you can imagine to Augusta National and Pine Valley, two of the greatest golf clubs in the world. I have teed it up at a tournament put on each November by the King of Morocco, been a part of countless charity outings, and frequently used golf as a business tool. What all that means is that I know the game — and those particular aspects of golf — from a variety of perspectives, which gives me a good base from which to write this opus.

Now, if only I could make my mustache twirl like Gary McCord's.

How This Book Is Organized

I've organized this book in a very simple fashion, beginning with explanations and descriptions of the rules, and then moving into the etiquette of the game. The book is divided into parts, which contain chapters that give you the information you're looking for. The following sections let you know what to expect from each part of the book.

Part 1: You've Got to Play by the Rules

The first part of this book covers the history of the rules; how, why, and when they were formed; and the people and organizations behind their development. I also explain why the game is so different from other sports, especially when it comes to following the rules. And I conclude the part with a description of 15 of the most important rules of golf, as well as some anecdotes of how golf rules have been interpreted in the past, usually to a player's great frustration.

Part II: The Unwritten Rules: How to Handle Yourself on (And off) the Course

No one has ever written an official book on golf etiquette, which means that knowing what to do and how to behave when you play the game is not always easy, especially for people just picking up the sport or who have learned on their own. This part, however, gives all golfers as good an understanding of those matters as they can get, beginning with play at three distinct types of venues and then covering business golf and tournament golf. I even get into betting a bit — and that's important because betting can be a very big, and very fun, part of golf. (In fact, many people who wouldn't even think of visiting a casino or playing a game of poker can't imagine enjoying themselves on the course without a little action on the side.)

Part III: Even More Rules . . . For Players and Spectators

More and more, golf has become a very useful tool for business or raising money for charity, and never before has the concept of outings been so popular. So in this section I tell you all about those sort of events and what you should — and should not — do when you play. Also, I give golf fans the lowdown on how to handle themselves at tournaments when they go to watch in person and answer all-important questions about getting autographs.

Part IV: The Part of Tens

I start this part with a list of the ten most devastating penalties. Then, for you weekend warriors, I provide a roster of the ten best games and bets to make in golf. And I finish the part with ten things you can learn about rules and etiquette from the movies — *Goldfinger, Caddyshack,* and *Tin Cup* among them.

Part V: Appendixes

No, I'm not talking about what a doctor takes out of your abdomen when you have shooting pains in your belly. Rather, appendixes are lists of things I think are essential to your having a better understanding of the rules and etiquette of the game. First off, I give you a glossary of golf terms, so you can understand all that is written about the game and talk like a real pro. Then I provide a list of resources, including names, addresses, phone numbers, and Web sites for the major organizations of golf as well as a number of local associations. The men and women who work at these organizations are always willing to help on issues of rules and etiquette, and many of them have various books, pamphlets, and videos available that deal with those subjects as well.

Icons Used in This Book

Icons are those attention-grabbing little pictures in the margins of this book that are intended to, well, grab your attention. Here are the icons I use in this book and an explanation of what each one means:

This icon steers you to important tips that will help you follow the rules of the game and conduct yourself with proper etiquette. Check it out.

As the robot in the old television series used to say, "Danger! Danger!" Be careful and pay heed when you see this icon nearby.

This information bears repeating. Bears repeating.

You don't have to be a nuclear physicist to understand the rules and etiquette of golf. But information like this just makes it seem that way.

This icon lets you know when I'm telling one of my best golf stories. So listen up!

Where to Go from Here

You don't have to read this book from cover to cover, like a novel, so pick the different chapters that interest you, and go from there. If you're a beginner, the Glossary may be an immediate help to you so that you have a better idea of how to talk golf before you start reading about it. Parts II and III, on the unwritten rules and etiquette, merits close attention for beginners as well. (Experience tells me that no matter how long you've been playing the game, looking over that material won't do you any harm. After all, we can all use a refresher course on occasion.) Chapter 3, which explains the rules themselves, will likely appeal to anyone heading out to the course, whether you're just playing on Sunday mornings with your buddies or competing in a tournament. Finally, if you use a lot of golf in your business, a number of the chapters will be helpful in that regard, especially Chapter 7, on outings and playing golf with your bosses and clients.

Part I

You've Got to Play by the Rules

The 5th Wave   By Rich Tennant

@RICHTENNANT

"Come on David, quit whining. You knew we enact stiff penalties for rule infractions at this club."

In this part . . .

*H*ere you'll find all the information you need on the rules of the game of golf — from where the game and its rules originated to the most controversial rule today.

Chapter 1

We Didn't Make the Rules

In This Chapter

▶ Rules 101: Getting a brief history of how the rules started

▶ Finding out the who, what, when, where, and why behind the rules

▶ Figuring out the roles played by the two major golf organizations: the USGA and the R&A

*W*e didn't make the rules, and our grandfathers didn't either. But a bunch of Scotsmen in the old country put together the first code back in the mid-1770s, when America was still a colony and Tiger was just a wild animal that roamed the Indian subcontinent. And ever since then, people who have swatted balls around grassy fields with clubs have had a set of rules and regulations to follow as they played the game called golf. Read on, you get a better sense of those do's and don'ts. I help you understand where those edicts came from, who made them up, and why they are so important to follow. I also show you how they have broken many a player's heart over the years, not because I take pleasure in the suffering of others, but because the rules of golf — and their strictest interpretations — will do that sometimes.

Taking a Brief Historical Glance at the Rules of Golf

The original rules of the game were written in 1744 by a club known as The Gentlemen Golfers of Leith and contained 13 "Articles & Laws in the Playing at Golf." Ten years later, they were adopted by The Society of St. Andrews Golfers — better known today as the Royal & Ancient Golf Club of St. Andrews, or simply the R&A — and they were, in all their 18th-century charm, as follows:

I. You must Tee your Ball within a Club length of the Hole.

II. Your Tee must be upon the ground.

III. You are not to change the Ball which you strike off the Tee.

IV. You are not to remove Stones, Bones or any Break-club for the sake of playing your Ball, except upon the fair Green, and that only within a Club length of your Ball.

V. If your Ball come among Watter, or any Wattery filth, you are at liberty to take out your Ball and throw it behind the hazard, six yards at least; you may play it with any club and allow your Adversary a stroke for getting out your Ball.

VI. If your Balls be found anywhere touching one another, you are to lift the first Ball till you play the last.

VII. At holing, you are to play your Ball honestly for the Hole, and not to play upon your Adversary's Ball, not lying in your way to the hole.

VIII. If you should lose your Ball by it being taken up, or in any other way, you are to go back to the spot where you struck last, and drop another Ball, and allow your Adversary a stroke for the misfortune.

IX. No man, at Holing his Ball, is to be allowed to mark to the Hole with his club or anything else.

X. If a Ball be stop'd by any person, Horse, Dog, or anything else, the Ball so stopped must be played where it lies.

XI. If you draw your Club in order to strike, and proceed so far in the stroke as to be bringing down your Club — if then your Club should break in any way, it is to be accounted a stroke.

XII. He whose Ball lyes further from the Hole is obliged to play first.

XIII. Neither Trench, Ditch nor Dyke made for the preservation of the Links, nor the Scholars' holes, nor the Soldiers' lines, shall be accounted a Hazard, but the Ball is to be taken out, Teed, and played with any iron Club.

As this language indicates, these rules were designed for match play and the consequences were very simple: If you violated any part of the code, you lost the hole and moved on to the next tee. Golfers in those days were insistent on playing the ball "as it lay," and if for some reason they were not able to do that, they lost the hole.

This list is of great historical interest and significance to anyone who enjoys playing the game. And it is also a hoot to go over when you consider some of the wording and, of course, the rules themselves. For example, what type of "Bones" are the folks from Leith talking about in Rule IV? I hope they're not referring to anything that would have come from a human being. And how about the word "Break-club"? Would anyone have known that that refers to a large pebble or obstacle? We also like the use of the term "Wattery Filth," which is how folks back then described the slime left by a receding tide. "Adversary" seems a quaint way to identify one's opponent, and we are glad there was a provision should a ball be "stopp'd by any person, Horse or Dog." (I'm sure we all see horses on our golf courses all the time.)

And how could a player not love Rule VI, which eventually became the "stymie" rule. The rule meant that whenever your opponent's ball lay between your ball and the hole, you couldn't ask him to mark his ball. In other words, you had to find a way around it, which often meant chipping your ball over his, or hitting yours to one side and then finishing it up. Talk about making the game more difficult. . . .

Figuring Out How, When, and Why the Rules Were Formed

No one can say for certain when the game of golf was actually founded. It is known, however, that the sport was popular among residents of St. Andrews — the site of Scotland's first university, the final resting place of the country's patron saint, and a one-time religious center — as far back as the early 1400s. In fact, golf had gained such popularity in that ancient city that James II banned it, together with European football, because young men from that area were said to be neglecting their archery practice in favor of those sports. And how many barbarians could a good Scotsman slay with a *mashie niblick* (a 7-iron)?

Golf did not having an official code of rules until the Golfers of Leith (who later became known as the Honourable Company of Edinburgh Golfers) got together in 1744. And it was another ten years before The Society of St. Andrews Golfers adopted those rules themselves, making only one minor change of procedure in the process. So like life back in those rough-and-tumble times, golf was a pretty chaotic undertaking. And it didn't seem to matter very much to players whether you could remove "Bones" or not.

But the Anglo-Saxons, it seemed, liked order above most everything else, and in time, that code of St. Andrews was adopted. As the game evolved in the late 18th century, many players and clubs did indeed follow those regulations. But a number of places were still making up their own rules. Even so, the group from St. Andrews eventually became acknowledged as the leading authority on the game, and in an 1812 meeting it created a revamped code by which the game should be played. Called the "Regulations for the Game of Golf," it included a total of 27 specific rules, some of which had been part of the original list. But many of those regulations were new, and they dealt with a variety of interesting issues, such as what to do when your ball lies in "Rabbit-scrape" or what happens if your ball hits your "adversary's caddy." A personal favorite is the one that reads: "WHEN a ball is completely covered with fog, bent, whins &c. so much thereof shall be set aside as that the Player shall have a full view of his Ball before he plays." (Personally, I have no idea what "bent" or "whins" are, nor can I be at all sure what that rule exactly means. Even my lawyer could write a clearer sentence.)

Diff'rent strokes: The R&A and the USGA

Today, the members of the R&A and the USGA meet twice annually to discuss possible rule changes. They copublish *The Official Rules of Golf,* and they do, for the most part, see eye to eye on matters. But it is important to understand that they have more than their fair share of differences as well. Consider, for example, the fact that for decades the R&A allowed usage of a golf ball that was smaller than the one used in the U.S. The difference in size was minuscule, but it took an extraordinary amount of time and effort before it was decided in 1990 that there could be only one legal-sized ball. And the smaller version disappeared from play.

An even more contentious issue between the two organizations is causing problems today, and that involves the so-called problem of "spring-like effect." The USGA says that the thin-faced titanium drivers that have been popularized by club makers such as Ely Callaway are letting golfers hit balls farther than ever before because they act as a sort of trampoline. And the USGA worries that that development threatens the integrity of traditional golf courses and is bad for the game. In fact, it thinks these clubs are so bad that they have instituted a special test for "spring-like effect" and created a list of clubs that do not pass that test, a sort of FBI Most Wanted List for club makers.

The R&A, on the other hand, does not believe "spring-like effect" is any problem at all, and it has decided not to test clubs for that characteristic. As a result, golf clubs that are considered by the USGA to be illegal for use in the States are perfectly allowable for competition in other parts of the world.

This is a development that only came to pass in the year 2000, and it has created perhaps the greatest schism between those two organizations in their existence. How or when it gets resolved remains to be seen, but one thing is clear: The longer that difference exists, the greater the confusion it causes and the more it threatens the joint credibility and strength of the two associations.

Interest in developing — and clarifying — such regulations grew, and by the end of the 19th century, the R&A, as the club was then officially known, created a Rules of Golf Committee and soon after developed a new unified code that contained many of the variations that have been applied in other golfing clubs throughout the British Isles. That move came largely in response to continued growth and development of the game and an increasing need for an overall rules authority. And when it happened, the R&A became one of the governing bodies of the game of golf, a position it still holds today.

Shortly before the R&A formed that committee in the United Kingdom, a group of golf clubs in America banded together to start the United States Golf Association (USGA). The necessity of that move was born out of disputes that arose in the early 1890s over national amateur championships that were held at two different venues, and it became clear to devotees of the sport that an impartial governing body was needed. Delegates from five different American clubs met in New York City on December 22, 1894, and the USGA was born.

As a matter of course, the USGA served to govern golf in the United States and Mexico, whereas the rest of the world followed the R&A (though it must be stated that Canada is self-governing but affiliated with the Scottish body). The two organizations have worked closely together from almost the beginning, with the USGA enjoying representation on the Rules of Golf Committee starting in 1907. But during the early part of the last century, the R&A and the USGA started to drift apart, and it soon became clear that something needed to be done. So representatives of both bodies — as well as people from golf associations in Canada and Australia — met in a committee room in London's House of Lords in 1951. And after much debate, they produced a unified code of rules that came to be used throughout the world of golf.

Recognizing the People and Organizations Who Developed and Enforced the Rules

Two primary organizations are in charge of making — and enforcing — the rules of golf: the Royal & Ancient Golf Club of St. Andrews (commonly called the R&A) and the United States Golf Association. The R&A is based in St. Andrews, Scotland, whereas its American counterpart is headquartered in Far Hills, New Jersey. Both organizations are run by men and women who devote untold hours to the game of golf, often take themselves quite seriously, and own an inordinate number of blue Brooks Brothers blazers (if they reside in the New World) or tweed jackets (if their base of operations lies on the other side of the pond). Some observers say that most members of those groups appear to be a little uptight, far removed from the regular golf scene, and a bit carried away with the power and prestige of their positions. And those characterizations are not entirely inaccurate. But we should also give those folks proper credit for caring enough about the game to become so involved and put in so much volunteer time. After all, these people spend hours on the job, and they receive very little in return.

The R&A

The formation of the organization that became the R&A came about for two primary reasons. Back in the mid-18th century, a handful of St. Andrews residents wanted to create a private golf club so that they could better enjoy the sport and the camaraderie the game so often nurtured among its practitioners, both on and off the course. Those same people, who were known as "22 Noblemen and Gentlemen of the Kingdom of Fife," also wanted to create an annual contest for a golf trophy that they hoped would establish St. Andrews as the home of the sport and help restore the significance and importance it enjoyed in years gone by when royalty and religious leaders frequently visited the seaside community. The Reformation, it seems, had taken some of the spiritual sheen away from the town, the huge cathedral once attended by Robert the Bruce lay in ruins, and the underfunded university was in danger of being moved. When all else fails, they seemed to think, the best thing to do was turn to golf.

So those men set up their club, and the first written record of their society reads:

> "the Noblemen and Gentlemen above named being admired of the Ancient and healthful exercise of the Golf, and at the same time having the interest and prosperity of the ancient city of St. Andrews at heart, being the Alma Mater of the Golf, did in the year of our Lord 1754 contribute for a Silver club having a St. Andrew engraved on the head thereof to be played for the Links of St. Andrews upon the fourteenth day of May said year and yearly in time coming. . . ."

In essence, the founders of the R&A were merely following the lead of the Gentlemen Golfers of Leith, which is considered to be the world's oldest golf club. But that initial group never gained the prominence of the R&A largely because they had to move several times in search of less crowded playing conditions than the five holes they had had at Leith. That lack of continuity and cohesion, combined with the growing strength of the duffers from St. Andrews, helped make the upstart organization of the R&A the major player that it is today. (It also didn't hurt that King William IV granted royal patronage to the R&A in 1834.)

Today, the R&A has three areas of responsibility:

✔ It administers the Official Rules of Golf.

✔ It runs the Open Championship, better known in the States as the British Open, as well as several other key professional and amateur competitions.

✔ It operates a private club with almost 2,400 members.

The organization is run by a network of committees, and it uses the funds garnered from running the highly profitable Open to finance a number of golf initiatives around the world, especially for juniors. It also contributes a great deal of time and money toward the advancement of golf course maintenance and conservation.

The USGA

The USGA, of course, is a much younger association, born at a New York City dinner party a few days before Christmas in 1894. The impetus for that gathering — which included delegates from the Newport (Rhode Island) Golf Club; the Shinnecock Hills Golf Club of Southampton, New York; The Country Club of Brookline, Massachusetts; the Chicago Golf Club; and the St. Andrew's Golf Club in Hastings-on-Hudson, New York — came from a dispute that had arisen that year over the crowning of a national amateur champion. Both St. Andrew's and Newport had staged invitational tournaments, and each declared its winner to be the amateur champ. The ensuing controversy made it clear to the powers of golf, which was just becoming popular in the U.S., that a governing body was needed not only to run both professional and amateur championships on a national level but also to administer the rules of the game. The end result of that dinner was the USGA, and Theodore A. Havemeyer was elected its first president. The next year, the association staged both the U.S. Open and U.S. Amateur Championships at Newport. And a month after those events, which were played on consecutive days in October 1895, the first U.S. Women's Amateur was played at the Meadow Brook Club in Hempstead, New York.

Not surprisingly, the USGA has grown quite a bit since then. Today, it represents more than 9,000 clubs and courses as well as some 800,000 individuals and boasts more than $200 million in assets. It is run, for all intents and purposes, by a 15-member Executive Committee. And more than 30 committees, comprised of approximately 1,300 men and women volunteers, help out.

One of the USGA's primary duties is the staging of national championships. It now puts on a total of 13, including the original three, and they are intended to cater to the widest possible range of golfers. There is, for example, the U.S. Amateur Public Links, which is for public course players, and the U.S. Mid-Amateur, which is for amateur competitors above the age of 25. It also has events for boys and girls, as well as for seniors. In addition, the USGA conducts the Walker Cup in cooperation with the R&A, and that biennial match, which was first held in 1922, pits players from the States against a team from Great Britain and Ireland. A similar competition for women, called the Curtis Cup, was started 10 years later.

But competitions are only part of what the USGA does. Rules are of primary importance as well, and the organization works with the R&A not only to make new ones — and new amendments — but also to help interpret and enforce them. In addition, the USGA is the administrator of the handicap system, which allows golfers of different abilities to compete against each other on relatively equal terms. It works hard to improve course conditioning and maintenance throughout its domain by conducting research, funding projects of that kind, disseminating information on greens-keeping, and running education programs. The association also operates an extensive research and test facility for clubs and balls, primarily to ensure (in its mind) that the traditional character of the game is not radically changed by the introduction of new equipment. It also rules on the amateur status of players and runs the USGA Museum and Library (holding 13,000 volumes) at its head-quarters in Far Hills, New Jersey.

Understanding the Importance of Knowing and Following the Rules

I don't know of any sport where the rules that govern it are so valued — and followed so closely — by the people who play it as they are in golf. The rules are one of the things that makes golf great, and makes it unique. And there is no other game in which self-policing of those rules are so critical and inherent to the game itself.

Take a sport like baseball. Think of the stories about pitchers scuffing up balls before they pitch them, or outfielders knowingly trapping a line drive and doing all they can to fool the umpire into thinking that they actually made the catch. Ever see a base runner who knew he was tagged out on his way into second base but was ruled safe anyway turn to the umpire and say, "I'm sorry, but I was out. I am going back to the dugout now"? The answer is no, because that sort of attitude doesn't exist in baseball. Instead, the idea, oftentimes, is "try to get away with as much as possible."

But you can't do that in golf. Your ball moves as you get ready to hit it out of the rough, and you must call the penalty on yourself. You inadvertently ground your club in a hazard, and you call that, too, even though no one may have seen you. "You do that because the rules are sacred in this game," says Joseph Cantwell, a longtime rules official and former president of the Metropolitan Golf Association outside New York City. "They are one of the things that separates it from other sports. They permeate the entire game, and the attitude of the players. They make golf what it is in many ways, because they are there and because people follow them so closely. People who play golf expect that sort of behavior and attitude from themselves and from the people they are playing with. The bottom line is, they all want to know that they are playing by the same rules. And they want to make sure they follow them."

So make sure you know the rules. No one can be expected to recite and understand all 34 rules and their various subsets and appendixes. But read about them. Talk about them. Try to understand them. And make sure you follow them. The game — and the people who play it — demand at least that much from you.

It's this simple: If you don't follow the rules, you are cheating, and cheating is like the scarlet letter in golf. There are a number of touring pros who have at one point in their life been accused of playing a little fast and loose with the rules during a tournament. People have said they didn't mark their balls carefully on the green or moved a stone or leaf from a hazard. And whether those allegations were fair or not, they have dogged those players for the rest of their careers.

I also know of regular weekend hackers who have gone to local country clubs to play in member-guest tournaments and were accused somewhere along the way of not following the letter of the law when it came to completing their rounds. And they were told in no uncertain terms that they were not welcome back. Ever. The moral here is that no sport takes its rules so seriously as golf.

The ten biggest milestones in rule-making

1744 — The first code of rules is written, by the Gentlemen Golfers of Leith, later to be known as the Honourable Company of Edinburgh Golfers. Ten years later, the Society of St. Andrews Golfers, adopts those regulations with only one minor change of procedure. In time, that group will become known as The Royal & Ancient Golf Club of St. Andrews and evolve into one of the primary governing bodies of golf. (In time, its members will also amass one of the greatest collections of single malt scotch anywhere.)

1894 — The United States Golf Association is founded.

1897 — The R&A forms the first Rules of Golf Committee.

1922 — Limits are imposed on the weight and size of golf balls for the first time, in an attempt to inhibit distance.

1929 — Steel shafts are permitted on clubs, signaling the demise of the hickory shaft. Tree lovers rejoice.

1939 — From this point on, players could carry only 14 clubs in their bags.

1952 — The first unified code of rules is agreed upon by the USGA and the R&A as well as golf associations from Australia and Canada. That same year, the quirky "stymie rule," which decreed that a golfer could not ask an opponent to mark his ball if it was in the way of his putt on the green and had to use other means to get over or around it, was abolished, much to the dismay of those who loved the havoc that regulation often wreaked.

1960 — Distance-measuring devices are banned. So much for "tape-measure" drives.

1990 — The 1.68-inch ball becomes the only legal ball, and the smaller "British" ball quickly goes out of style.

1998 — The USGA begins testing clubs for "spring-like effect," a move that stirs the ire of equipment makers, confuses consumers, and leads to the introduction of so-called *outlaw drivers* that do not conform to association regulations. It also creates a breach between the USGA and the R&A and lots of murky thoughts on how the Official Rules of Golf should be applied. Even Arnold Palmer gets into the act, saying he has no problem using one of those non-conforming boomers when he plays casual rounds of golf with friends. Golf traditionalists, as well as most USGA leaders, are shocked.

Taking a Look at the Best and Worst of the Rules

Though I believe in strict adherence to the rules of golf, I do have my opinions about which ones makes the most — or least — sense. So I give you the best and worst the game has to offer in this section.

The five best rules in golf

Actually, I really should describe these as five *of the best* rules in golf, because it really is hard to single out any as being that much better than the others. But I like these most of all and feel that golfers should pay special heed to them.

- **Rule 1:** According to this rule, you must play the same ball from the teeing ground into the hole. No fair driving with a distance ball, then switching to a softer one that spins better for your approach shot. The only exceptions are under Rule 5-3, which allows a player to change his ball should it become visibly cut, cracked, or otherwise "unfit for play."

- **Rule 3-4:** The rule reads as follows: "If a competitor refuses to comply with a Rule affecting the rights of another competitor, he shall be disqualified." This has to do with stroke play, when it is the total score for the round that counts. And it means that everybody, and I mean everybody, must be considerate of their opponent and play by the rules. If someone doesn't, he is done.

- **Rule 6-5:** This rule says you are responsible for playing your own ball. Put an identification mark on it to be sure (see Figure 1-1). For some of my friends, that's like elementary school art class, and they enjoy decorating their Top Flites and Maxflis with various dots and initials. The colors and designs may be different, but the intent is just the same: Make it easy to make sure you have hit your ball. If you don't and, say, hit your opponent's, then it's loss of the hole in match play and a two shot penalty in stroke play.

- **Rule 10a:** According to this rule, the side that has the honor at the first teeing ground is determined by the order of the draw. The side that wins a hole takes the honor at the next teeing ground. If a hole has been halved, the side that had the honor at the previous teeing ground retains it. I like this rule because having the honor on the tee means you have just won a hole, and the longer you keep it, the better you feel. It's a constant reminder to you, and anyone who can see you play, that you are on top, and you want to stay that way as long as you can. There are even betting games that earn you points — and ultimately some extra cash — for having the honors most often during a match.

> ✔ **Rule 28:** This rule indicates that if your ball is unplayable, you have three options. You can either play it from where you hit your last shot; drop it within two club lengths of where your ball is now, no closer to the hole; or keep the point where the ball is between you and the hole and drop a ball on that line. (You can go back as far as you want.) And it's important because we *all* have unplayable-lie problems.

Oh, and before I go, there is one more rule to keep in mind: Make sure to have fun whenever you head out to the course.

Give your ball an identifying mark.

Figure 1-1: So you know it's yours . . .

The five dumbest rules in golf

I should qualify this to mean the five dumbest interpretations of the rules, because who am I to say that any of golf's 34 rules are dumb? But sometimes the way they are enforced can be incredibly stupid or ridiculous because players, spectators, and officials lose all common sense and insist on the strictest of applications, even when there is no attempt to cheat or circumvent. And it drives me more than a little crazy when that happens.

> ✔ **Rule 19-2a:** Consider, for example, this incident during the 1979 English Amateur Championship. Golfer Reg Gladding drove his ball into the top of a bunker during a closely contested match, and fearful that he would start an avalanche of sand if he stepped in from the top, chose to enter the hazard from below, carefully taking his stance. During his swing, however, he lost his balance

and fell backwards head over heels to the bottom of the bunker. (Remember: No one ever said you had to be an athlete to play this game.) Sand came pouring down after him, and so did his ball, striking him in the back. And according to Rule 19-2a, which states that if a player's ball is accidentally deflected or stopped by himself, his partner, or either of their caddies or equipment, he shall lose the hole, Gladding not only lost face but also the hole (and ultimately the match).

✔ **Rule 13-4:** Longtime touring pro Paul Azinger was playing in the Doral tournament in Florida in 1996 when he got ready to take a shot from the inside edge of the lake on the final hole. Just before he started to swing, he kicked a rock out of his way while taking his stance. And sure enough, some television viewer phoned in to say that he had violated the rule for not "moving loose impediments in a hazard" (Rule 13-4). Azinger didn't think he had done anything wrong and went ahead and signed his scorecard when he was done. But after officials considered the unsolicited phone call, he was disqualified.

✔ **Rule 13-3:** A similar thing happened to Craig Stadler in San Diego in 1997 when he laid down a towel to hit a shot underneath a tree from his knees. Again, a fan called in after seeing what had happened on TV, accusing Stadler of violating Rule 13-3, which says a player may not build a stance. Of course, the one known as The Walrus didn't think he had done anything wrong, so he went ahead and signed his scorecard when he was done playing. After all, he was only trying to keep his pants from getting dirty. But when the rules officials learned of the phone call and the viewer's point, they felt they had no choice but to disqualify the man.

✔ **Rule 6-4:** Mark Johnson had an 11-shot lead during the final round of the 2000 Arizona Mid-Amateur when disaster struck. It was Father's Day, and coincidentally his son Seth's 14th birthday, and he had asked Seth to caddie for him that morning. Seth had brought along a friend, Derek Harris, and everything seemed fine on the third hole when Seth pulled a putter out of his bag, handed it to Derek who, in turn, handed it to Johnson. Johnson knew immediately that something was wrong, and he quickly turned to an Arizona Golf Association official and asked, "How many?", as in how many strokes would he be penalized for having "two caddies," which is against the rules. But the official shook his head and gave his decision: disqualification.

✔ **Rule 4-4a:** Two friends of mine were playing in the club championship at their course one September day. They both had the same caddie, who was carrying double. And because they both bought their equipment from the head professional there, they had the same color and type of bag and irons. Even the head covers for their woods looked similar. The match was tied after three holes, and the players stepped to the tee of the 4th, a short, scenic par-3 that requires a carry over water. The fellow who had the honor took a quick look at the flag to judge the direction and strength of the wind and then asked the caddie for an 8-iron. The caddie complied, and my friend took his shot, nestling his ball just a few feet from the pin. He was quite pleased with his efforts until his opponent said he had played that shot with *his* club (because the caddie had inadvertently reached into the wrong bag). And as a result of Rule 4-4a, which decrees that a player may only use one of the 14 clubs that he selected at the start of the round, he lost the hole.

The most controversial rule in golf today

The most controversial rule in golf today would be Rule 4-1a, which relates to the design and manufacture of clubs. Basically, all it says is that players must use clubs that "conform with this Rule and the provisions, specifications and interpretations set forth in Appendix II." Simple enough, right? Not really, and if you examine Appendix II, 5a, you will see why. It's the one that reads, "The material and construction of, or any treatment to, the face or club head shall not have the effect at impact of a spring (test on file). . . . " And that rule has caused more problems than a snap-hook into a crowded gallery.

The problems with what is known as "spring-like effect" began to surface in the mid-1990s, when members of the USGA hierarchy started hearing stories about high-tech drivers being built in Japan with incredibly thin faces that acted as a sort of catapult with balls. Their fear was seated not only in what was currently available in the Far East but also in what technological advancements may be coming down the road. So the association decided to take action in the form of developing a test, and if a club exceeded a limit for what is called a *coefficient of resolution,* or spring-like effect, then it was deemed nonconforming.

It didn't take long for news of that move to get around the golf community, and equipment makers were, for the most part, horrified. In May 1998, Callaway Golf, which has made most of its millions on oversized, titanium-head drivers known as Big Berthas and Great Big Berthas that added both distance and control to most every golfer's game, began warning retailers and consumers of what it characterized as a campaign to deprive the golfing masses of game-enhancing features of club design (and them of much-desired profits). About that same time, then USGA president F. Morgan "Buzz" Taylor began explaining his organization's side of things — and combatively fueling the debate fire — by saying that the USGA's mission was to "preserve and protect the game's ancient and honorable traditions . . . and there is not one lawyer in the world who is going to get in our way of doing that."

The next month, at the U.S. Open in San Francisco, the USGA formally announced its proposal to test for spring-like effect. Other equipment makers, notably the people at Acushnet Company, which makes Titleist balls and clubs among other products, began questioning the USGA's intentions and also its logic. Acushnet's argument was that spring-like effect was a non-issue, and a little bit more distance off the tee was by no means bad for the game. If anything, the thinking went, it would help bring more people into the game (and help manufacturers more fully recover from what had been a series of tough years at the end of the 1990s). Later in the fall of 1998, the USGA decided to approve its test for spring-like effect, and when it released its first list of nonconforming drivers, a new offering from Callaway, called the ERC, was on the list.

As the USGA tried to explain its rationale for the spring-like effect testing, the R&A remained strangely quiet and declined to take a stand on the issue. Its official line was that it was unconvinced the phenomenon even existed and felt that more research was in order before any conclusions could be drawn. (Unofficially, the R&A said it had to proceed with great caution so as not to provoke charges of collusion with the USGA and restraint of trade, which might result in costly antitrust litigation with equipment makers.)

While the R&A continued to study the issue, Callaway, which is among the largest and most prominent of the clubmakers and has produced some of the most popular drivers in history, began to exploit the difference of opinion by aggressively marketing its ERC driver in Japan and Europe (where the R&A, and not the USGA, is the ruling authority). The club was very well received, and a number of pros on both those tours start using the club. Although it was not officially being sold directly in the U.S., hundreds of ERCs began finding their way into America through the gray market, usually for prices exceeding $1,000.

This split between the two organizations concerned many industry observers, and they worried about the confusion and controversy that could arise with two sets of rules in place. But most expected the matter to be resolved in rather short order, with the R&A coming over to the side of its American counterpart and at the very least endorsing its fears over spring-like effect, if not the actual mode of testing. But the R&A surprised most everybody in golf by deciding in the fall of 2000 not to test clubs for that condition and concluded that the current generation of thin-faced drivers do not pose a threat to the game.

The fallout from that decision — and the one the USGA unilaterally made in 1998 — has been huge. In the countries that follow the R&A, the issue of spring-like effect does not exist, and therefore there are not any restrictions on clubs like the ERC. But in the realm of the USGA, which includes the United States and Mexico, the spring-like effect test is still in effect, and clubs that do not pass, like the ERC, are considered illegal and not to be used. That includes the PGA Tour, of course, any club or local event where USGA rules apply, and, technically, any round of golf where a score is going to be turned in for USGA handicap purposes (more on that in Chapter 4).

But the use of the ERC is not going to be easy to police or handle. First of all, there were already a number of "gray market" ERCs in the U.S. when the R&A announced its decision on spring-like effect. And a number of lesser companies were making models of their own. But as shortly after it heard about the R&A's ruling, Callaway said it would begin selling a new driver in the U.S. that does not conform to USGA regulations, and it enlisted none other than Arnold Palmer to endorse that move and the fact that it was fine to use a conforming club in tournament play and a nonconforming one at other times. In addition, several other major manufacturers said that as a matter of survival, they, too, would have to develop and bring to market nonconforming clubs of their own.

To some people, that is not such a big deal, and they buy into Palmer's argument that as long as the clubs are not being used in tournament play, they are all right. But to many others, myself included, that really misses the point. As it stands now, nonconforming clubs are against the rules, whether you are playing in the Masters or enjoying a four-ball match among friends on a Sunday morning. So playing with them is, in essence, breaking the rules (because USGA rules govern all play in the States). If you use a nonconforming club, you are cheating. And cheating with an illegal club is really no different than teeing a ball up in the fairway or grounding your club in a bunker.

That's where all the debate has come from on this issue of spring-like effect, and it is certain to continue for a while. Maybe the USGA made a bad rule with its test for spring-like effect. Maybe that needs to be changed (my thought is that it should be as soon as possible). But until it is, the rules of the game as they stand have to be observed. If they are not, then you are not really playing golf.

Chapter 2

It's Not Just a Game (Why Golfers Are So Devoted to Golf)

● ●

In This Chapter

▶ Knowing why golfers are a dedicated bunch

▶ Identifying how golf is different from any other sport

▶ Making a few pleas for common sense

● ●

1 was driving by the Connecticut golf club I belong to the other day and was momentarily stunned by what I saw. The temperature was down in the mid-40s, the wind was blowing at least 25 knots, a chilly rain was beginning to fall, and there, on the course, were perhaps a dozen groups of players. All bundled up. Rain suits on. Knit caps on their heads. Umbrellas out. And still plugging away. Now, I consider myself something of a fanatic when it comes to the game of golf. But going out in such brutal fall weather? It seemed more than a little over-the-top to me.

Then I remembered a sand and rain storm I played in during a tournament in Morocco a couple of years ago that turned the sky an ugly purple and snapped branches off the cork trees that lined the course. I thought back to the morning I teed it up during a light snow a couple of springs ago. And I considered all the times my friends and I have braved cold, rain, and wind just to play a round, oftentimes, it seems, to the amusement of mallards who huddle in the corner of some water hazard and wonder what in the world we are doing out in weather that is even too rough for ducks. I went over in my head at least a dozen occasions over the past year or two when I headed out to play in what had to be considered extreme conditions, when I had to wear gloves on my hands and put two pairs of socks on my feet. And suddenly, those people I saw out on the links that afternoon didn't seem so crazy at all.

Actually, they were just acting like golfers. Most of us are that way about the game. We wait in line for hours to get on a good public course. Or we pay thousands of dollars a year to belong to a club where we can play regularly and bring our friends. We spend insane amounts of money on equipment and lessons, and we travel to the far corners of the earth for a chance to tee it up on classic courses. We strain marriages, test relationships, and risk jobs because we don't know how we could really survive without our Saturday and Sunday morning rounds or the quick 18 holes we sneak out for in the middle of the week. We endure even the most horrendous shots and conditions because, as the saying goes, a bad day of golf is always better than a good day at the office — or just about anything else, for that matter. As Hall of Fame musician and longtime golfer Willie Nelson once told me: "There aren't many things I like better than a game of golf, and like sex, it's one of those things you don't have to be very good at to enjoy. Somebody likes every shot."

Another example of golfers' devotion to the game is the way in which most players follow the rules. Yes, there are cheaters in the sport like there are cheaters everywhere. But I know of no other game where players put so much credence into the code that guides it. I have even found that people who would rip off their grandmothers to make an extra buck in a business deal and have no qualms about stiffing the Internal Revenue Service for thousands of dollars of unreported income every year wouldn't even consider kicking a ball out of the rough or using an illegal club. I have seen guys who are famous for telling the tallest of tales become George Washington and Abe Lincoln all rolled into one when they are out on the golf course. The very nature of the game demands that devotion to the rules, and the vast majority of people who play gladly adhere to them with almost religious fervor. It's as if they worry they will be banished to Hades if they don't abide.

Why Golf Is Different from Other Sports

Golf is different for a lot of reasons, but the most significant and obvious one is devotion to the rules. Consider, for example, a group of guys playing touch football on a crisp autumn afternoon. Obviously, certain basic rules apply, but no one is really concerned about a player moving before the snap, or whether someone holds a member of the other team as he tries to rush the passer. No one is going to take back a touchdown because he may have pushed off on an opponent as he was running a pass pattern. In fact, people usually try to get away with as much as they can in order to win.

I know that because I have played more than my fair share of touch football over the years. And the same thing holds true in basketball, baseball or hockey. There is a sense of casualness, of relaxation, of letting things go sometimes just because it is a pickup game, and the rules simply aren't applied as diligently as they may be professionally. Even if you play in organized sports leagues, you will likely find yourself — and others — doing what it takes to win, no matter if you have to sneak in an elbow here or a clip there. And take a look at the professional games. What National Football League offensive lineman hasn't held on dozens of plays during a game? And isn't he proud of the fact that he gets away with it all? What National Hockey League player hasn't speared his opponent with his stick when the referee wasn't looking? Or smeared his face with his glove. What National Basketball Association forward hasn't mugged an opposing player under the boards several times in a game just to get a rebound? That sort of behavior and attitude, quite frankly, is part of those sports.

But it is not part of golf. The rules in golf are followed as closely during a Sunday morning match between friends as they are in the final round of the Masters. Or at least they are expected to be. There is no room for fudging, and to turn your nose up at the rules of golf is to turn your nose up at the game itself. Why play if you are not going to abide by the rules? There is no glory for the one who cheats, no pats on the back for getting the job done at the expense of the rules. You face only ridicule and humiliation if your transgressions are found out — and unless you have no conscience at all, lots of sleepless nights if you are the only one who knows.

To illustrate that remarkable difference between golf and other sports, a good friend relates a story about the time a childhood neighbor played in his first tournament. The young man was a terrific high school athlete who had excelled in football and baseball, and partway through his teens, he got interested in playing golf. He took a few lessons and picked the sport up so quickly that he was asked to play for his school team. On the first hole of his first match, he sliced a ball into the woods and went in there with his partner to find it. The boy quickly located the ball and thought nothing of picking it up from the ground, wiping it off with a towel and then sticking it on a tee he has placed in the ground. Of course, he was supposed to play the ball exactly as it laid, and his partner was horrified. "What are you doing?" he asked, amazed that his friend could break so many rules in such a short period of time. And the young man wasn't the least bit taken aback. "No one is watching," he replied. "What does it matter?" His friend shook his head. "It matters a lot," he said. "This is golf. You can't cheat in golf the way you can in football or baseball."

Another way that golf is different is that it is just about the only sport that is played without an umpire or referee. Sure, there are officials available at all professional tournaments (and major amateur competitions) to help interpret the rules. But they are not there to make sure the competitors don't cheat. That's up to the players themselves.

And in what other sport do players call their own penalties, no matter what the consequences? PGA touring pros have taken themselves completely out of contention in tournaments because they felt they violated some rule of the game, no matter how innocent the infraction may have been. They may have watched their ball move inadvertently as they got ready to hit it, or attested the wrong score on their card, or taken just a few seconds too long to find a ball they feared was lost. And though no one else may have seen or been aware of the transgression, the players still took it upon themselves to call a penalty, even if the move cost them ten of thousands of dollars in prize money.

Look at what happened to Tom Kite during a tournament at the Pinehurst resort in North Carolina some years ago. A ball of his oscillated on the green and moved ever so slightly while he addressed it. No one saw it, but Kite called the penalty on himself anyway, and that one stroke ultimately cost him the tournament. (That same year, however, he won the USGA's Bob Jones Award, which is named after the great amateur golfer and given annually in recognition of distinguished sportsmanship in the game.)

Can you imagine Shaquille O'Neal calling a foul on himself in the last minute of play during Game Seven of the NBA playoffs? Or some World Series pitcher stopping play and admitting to the umpire that the last ball he threw shouldn't count because he loaded it up with Vaseline? No way. But that sort of thing happens in golf all the time.

The Devotion Players Have for the Rules That Govern Golf

It is nothing short of remarkable to see and hear how closely the vast majority of all players follow those rules, even if they don't agree with them. "I have been officiating at both national and regional golf tournaments for the past 15 years," says Joe Cantwell, the former president of the Metropolitan Golf Association outside New York city. "And I have seen players call penalties on themselves all the time. Their ball may move the slightest bit on the green once they've grounded their clubs, or perhaps when they are addressing it in the rough. They didn't mean for it to happen. They weren't trying to advance the ball, but it moved nonetheless. So they call a penalty, even if no one else has seen what they have. They don't hesitate to do it, because they know and understand that is the way to act."

Tom Graham is a top amateur golfer in the Metropolitan New York area and a competitor in the 1998 U.S. Senior Open. And he understands the torturous devotion players have to the rules of golf as well as anyone. (I say torturous because no one likes calling a penalty on himself, and some players have thought of doing themselves a terrible injury after something like that happens.) "I was playing in this team event in Westchester County one time, and I was getting ready to hit a wedge shot," Graham explained. "I looked down at the ball, then looked up at the green, and then back down at the ball. And when I looked down the second time, I touched the back of my ball with my club. It was more a nick than anything else, and the ball moved maybe a quarter of a revolution. No one saw it, and when I knocked it onto the green of this par-5 and 2-putted, my opponent said, 'Five, right?' And I said, 'No, I'm afraid that's a six. I had to take a penalty back there.' I wanted to scream I was so mad at myself. But there was really nothing else I could do."

Graham has also watched in horror as some of the best professional players had similar things happen to them. "I remember Hale Irwin going to hit a short putt at some big event several years ago," he recalled. "He grounded his putter and went to tap his ball in. But somehow, his putter got stuck in the green for a second, and he whiffed on the putt. Now, he, or anyone else, could have easily explained that that had been a practice swing, and no one would have been the wiser. But Irwin stood up to what had happened and took a stroke. And he lost the tournament as a result."

Interestingly, golfers demonstrate their devotion to the rules of the game in plenty of other ways as well. Witness all that has been going on with regards to "spring-like effect" and the decision by the Callaway Golf Company to sell a driver in the U.S. called the ERC II that does not conform to USGA regulations (but is legal in the R&A domain overseas). "If it does not conform to USGA rules, then I really don't want to sell it," said Jack Druga, the head professional at my home course, the Country Club of Fairfield. "We recently had a meeting among PGA professionals in our section, and there was a strong feeling against allowing these clubs to be used in club tournaments. If we say those are okay, then what about illegal balls or tees in the fairways? Where does it all stop? To us, the rules are paramount."

Several pros that I know agree with Druga's comments, and their feeling is that the rules are bigger than any profits they may make from an illegal club.

Child's play

One of my regular golfing buddies headed out to the first tee at his course one day to play a match against a good friend of his in the quarterfinals of their club championship. They both hit solid drives off the tee, followed those up with strong second shots, and after each of them 2-putted, they were ready to put down a pair of fours on the card. Hole halved, or as we golfers like to say, "No blood." But as my friend went to put his putter back in his bag, he saw that his 9-year-old's cutoff putter was mixed up with the rest of his clubs. According to Rule 4-4, a player may only have a maximum of 14 clubs, and counting the one used by his child, he now had 15. So he had no choice but to concede the previous hole to his opponent. And to protect himself from further penalty, he had to leave the extra putter on the bench by the second tee and return to pick it up later.

Another friend of mine, who is a product tester for Callaway on the basis of his being a strong amateur player, took it even one step further. "Callaway sent me a sample of that new ERCII driver, and I didn't even open the box," he said. "I just sent it right back to them because I have no interest in playing a driver that does not conform to USGA rules."

A Plea for Common Sense

I spend the better part of this book stressing the importance of playing by the rules whenever you step onto a golf course. And I'm not about to go back on that theme. But it is important to acknowledge that the rules we hold to be so dear can also be enforced in ways that are, shall I say, less than desirable. Officials can be overzealous. Players can be too tough — on themselves and on others. People can see only the black and white of the situation and not the gray. I'm not suggesting in any way that the rules should be bent. They are in place to protect each player, his competitor, and the game itself. But I'd like them to be enforced fairly. I would like to see some consideration given to intent. And I want to make sure that the rules are interpreted properly.

In Chapter 1, I relate a story about a man who was leading the Arizona Mid-Am and got disqualified when his son handed his putter to a friend, who in turned handed it to the father who was playing in the tournament. It was later discovered that there had been rulings in similar circumstances that did not become violations. So the official who ruled against the man didn't have to be draconian about the rules. After all, kids were involved, and no one was trying to cheat. The player was 11 strokes ahead when he was disqualified. I would argue that he should have been penalized a couple of strokes, but not disqualified.

The same could be said for an incident involving Craig Stadler and the towel he used to keep his pants from getting dirty. Does anyone really believe that he was trying to "build a stance," as the fellow who phoned in the violation to tournament officials after seeing it on TV said? Stadler was only trying to keep his pants clean. And how about that man who found his daughter's putter in his bag? If I were his opponent, I would thank him for bringing that situation to my attention, tell him to take the club out of his bag, and insist that he forget about conceding the first hole. There was clearly no intent there. The two of them belong to a family club, and he had just been tooling around the golf course with his daughter the day before. Why in the world should he lose a hole because of that?

I remember playing in a tournament at my club one day, and after hitting a very poor drive on our par-3 17th, I had to walk into a hazard to play a ball that was sitting on a sliver of beach that rose in something of an incline to the green. I took out my sand wedge and walked down to my ball. And on my way there, I tripped on a piece of imbedded driftwood and was about to tumble into the pond that guarded the front of the hole. But I saved myself by sticking out my sand wedge and using it like a cane to break my fall.

My opponent saw that and immediately accused me of grounding my club in the hazard. But according to the Rules of Golf, 13-4, Exceptions, a player is not to be penalized if he touches the ground in the hazard so long as "nothing is done which constitutes testing the condition of the hazard or improves the lie of the ball." And it specifically mentions "if the player touches the ground . . . as a result of or to prevent falling. . . ."

Now that's what I call common sense.

A Plea for TV Viewers to Put Down the Phone

Golf fans who tune in to professional tournaments on television have a nasty habit of calling in to the network on occasion when they think they see a rules violation and ratting out the pro involved. That's how Stadler got busted in San Diego. And that's how Paul Azinger got nailed at Doral (in an incident I discuss in Chapter 1). Now, I understand that those fans are well-intentioned, but my feeling is that they really need to leave the enforcement of the Rules of Golf to the players themselves and the officials on-site.

Two-time U.S. Open champion Curtis Strange recently wrote about that issue in one of the national golf publications. Strange feels it is flat-out wrong for those TV viewers to call. For one thing, he argues, it's not fair to the player who happens to be on camera while others are not under such scrutiny. Secondly, camera angles can be deceptive, and you can't always be certain that what you see on TV is exactly what you get in reality. To emphasize that point, Strange discussed the 2000 U.S. Open and a camera shot that appeared to show Tiger Woods marking his ball on a green inappropriately. But after looking at another camera angle, viewers saw he had indeed marked the ball the right way, and a potential brouhaha was defused.

Strange's main point is that the players are quite capable of policing themselves, and they do it very well. They do not need the unsolicited help of television viewers who may or may not know the rules, or be sure of what they have seen.

And there's another reason why those calls should be ignored: It's like tattling. Calling in is like being a know-it-all or a goody-goody. It's like sticking your nose into someplace where it doesn't belong.

If the tournament organizers had wanted another rules official, they would have called you. But they didn't. So put down the phone.

Give them two

The usual penalty for players victimized by call-ins is disqualification, because the officials generally don't get to hear the suggestion and interpret the rule until after the player has finished his round and signed his scorecard. And after a player has signed his scorecard, he can be disqualified for any discrepancies that are found there. Due to the fact that a rules violation entails a one- or two-stroke penalty at the very least, the player's score would then be deemed inaccurate, and he would be out of the event.

That sort of situation rankles professionals to no end, and a number of them have proposed solutions. One of those comes from one-time British Open champ Ian Baker-Finch, who feels that if a player inadvertently and unintentionally breaks a rule on the course and is unaware of that breach when he signs his card and turns it in, he should be given a two-stroke penalty as opposed to being DQed (in golf parlance, disqualified).

I like that solution, because it makes a lot of common sense.

Chapter 3

The Rules (And I'm Not Talking about Dating)

· ·

In This Chapter

▶ Getting the scoop on the most important rules in golf

▶ Seeing how the rules have been interpreted and enforced

▶ Taking a lesson from Willie Nelson

· ·

*T*he book is innocent-looking enough. But it can be a couple hundred pages of procedure, confusion, heartbreak, logic, clarity, and imperatives. It is *The Official Rules of Golf,* as approved by our friends at the United States Golf Association and the Royal & Ancient Golf Club of St. Andrews and updated every four years. (Call the USGA at 800-336-4446 to order your copy. And believe me, anyone who plays golf should have one.)

In actuality, there are only 34 rules of golf, so you have to wonder why a book that contains them ends up being so long. But golf does have its complications, and the book contains countless definitions, notes, subsections, interpretations, and other important information on how to play the game the right way.

And if *The Official Rules of Golf* isn't enough, there is also a companion publication known as *The Decisions of the Rules of Golf.* This is a collection of official rulings on over 1,000 golf situations, and is a must-read — and a must-have — for rules officials or anyone who is overseeing a tournament or match. (You may call the USGA to order a copy.) This manual was developed simply because the governing bodies of the game receive thousands of calls and letters each year seeking clarification of the rules — and the hope was that this book would help answer most of those questions. It covers everything, from dealing with relief situations and procedures to a player's responsibilities. There is even a section on "threesomes and foursomes." But remember, I said I'm not talking about dating here.

Fifteen of the Most Important Rules in Golf

Every rule in golf is important, and it is impossible to say one is any more critical than another. But I think the following bear special attention for those who are just learning about the game as well as for players who have been going at it for years (but never really bothered to read that little white book). So here they are, as they appear in *The Official Rules of Golf.*

Before you go any further, you may want to familiarize yourself with the definitions of terms that are included in Appendix A to make sure you understand every little nuance, because there are plenty.

Rule 1-1: The Game — General

The game of golf consists of playing a ball from what is called the *teeing ground* into the hole by a stroke or successive strokes in accordance with the rules. (And one of those rules is that you must play the same ball from the tee into the hole and change it only when allowed.)

Rule 2-1: The Match — Winner of Hole; Reckoning of Holes

In match play, the game is played by holes. Except as otherwise provided in the rules, a hole is won by the side that holes its ball in the fewest strokes. In a handicap match, the lower net score wins the hole.

The reckoning of holes is kept by the terms so many *holes up* or *all square* and so many *to play.*

A side is *dormie* when it is as many holes up as there are holes remaining to play. (The expression *dormie* is said to come from the French word *dormir,* which means to sleep. And that's what can sometimes happen to players who are up two holes, for example, with two to play. They can go right to sleep, and pretty soon the match is tied.)

Rules 3-1 and 3-2: Stroke play

3-1 — Winner: The competitor who plays the stipulated round or rounds in the fewest strokes is the winner.

3-2 — Failure to Hole Out: If a competitor fails to hole out at any hole and does not correct his mistake before he plays a stroke from the next teeing ground, or in the case of the last hole of the round, before he leaves the putting green, he shall be disqualified. (In other words, you must hole out on each hole.)

Rule 4-4: Clubs — Maximum of 14 Clubs

4-4a — Selection and Addition of Clubs: The player shall start a stipulated round with not more than 14 clubs. He is limited to the clubs thus selected for that round except that, if he started with fewer than 14 clubs, he may add any number provided his total number does not exceed 14. The addition of a club or clubs must not unduly delay play (Rule 6-7) and must not be made by borrowing any club selected for play by any other person playing on the course.

4-4b — Partners May Share Clubs: Partners may share clubs, provided that the total number of clubs carried by the partners so sharing does not exceed 14. (The penalty for breach of Rule 4-4a or 4-4b regardless of number of excess clubs carried is a maximum loss of two holes per round in match play, and four strokes per round in stroke play, depending on how many holes were played with the excess club.)

4-4c — Excess Club Declared Out of Play: Any club carried or used in breach of this rule shall be declared out of play by the player immediately upon discovery that a breach has occurred and thereafter shall not be used by the player during the round. (The penalty for breach of Rule 4-4c is disqualification.)

Rule 5-3: The Ball — Ball Unfit for Play

A ball is unfit for play if it is visibly cut, cracked, or out of shape (see Figure 3-1). A ball is not unfit for play solely because mud or other materials adhere to it, its surface is scratched or scraped, or its paint is damaged or discolored.

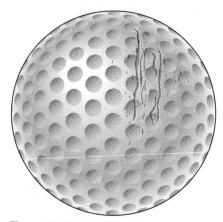

Figure 3-1: A ball that has been cut or cracked is unfit for play.

If a player has reason to believe his ball has become unfit for play during the play of the hole being played, he may during the play of such hole lift his ball without penalty to determine whether it is unfit.

Before lifting the ball, the player must announce his intention to his opponent in match play or his marker or a fellow competitor in stroke play and mark the position of the ball. He may then lift and examine the ball without cleaning it and must give his opponent, marker, or fellow-competitor an opportunity to examine the ball.

If he fails to comply with this procedure, he shall incur a penalty of one stroke.

If it is determined that the ball has become unfit for play during the play of the hole being played, the player may substitute another ball, placing it on the spot where the original ball lay. Otherwise, the original ball shall be replaced.

If a ball breaks into pieces as a result of a stroke, the stroke shall be canceled and the player shall play a ball without penalty as nearly as possible at the spot from which the original ball was played.

Rules 7-1 and 7-2: Practice

7-1 — Before or Between Rounds

7-1a — Match Play: On any day of a match play competition, a player may practice on the competition course before the round.

7-1b — Stroke Play: On any day of a stroke competition or playoff, a competitor shall not practice on the competition course or test the surface of any putting green on the course before a round or playoff. When two or more rounds of a stroke competition are to be played over consecutive days, practice between those rounds on any competition course remaining to be played, or testing the surface of any putting green on such course, is prohibited.

Exception: Practice putting or chipping on or near the first teeing ground before starting a round or playoff is permitted.

(The penalty for breach of rule 7-1b is disqualification.)

7-2 — During Round: A player shall not play a practice stroke either during the play of a hole or between the play of two holes except that, between the play of two holes, the player may practice putting or chipping on or near the putting green of the hole last played, any practice putting green or the teeing ground of the next hole to be played in the round, provided such practice stroke is not played from a hazard and does not unduly delay play.

Strokes played in continuing the play of a hole, the result of which has been decided, are not practice strokes.

(The penalty for breach of Rule 7-2 is loss of hole in match play and two strokes in stroke play.)

Note 1: A practice swing is not a practice stroke and may be taken at any place, provided the player does not breach the rules.

Rules 8-1 and 8-2: Advice; Indicating Line of Play

8-1 — Advice: During a stipulated round, a player shall not give advice to anyone in the competition except his partner and may ask for advice only from his partner or either of their caddies.

8-2 — Indicating Line of Play

8-2a — Other Than on Putting Green: Except on the putting green, a player may have the line of play indicated to him by anyone, but no one shall be positioned by the player or close to the line or an extension of the line beyond the hole while the stroke is being played. Any mark placed during the play of the hole by a player or with his knowledge to indicate the line shall be removed before the stroke is played.

Exception: Flagstick attended or held up (see Rule 17-1).

8-2b — On the Putting Green: When a player's ball is on the putting green, the player, his partner or either of their caddies may, before but not during the stroke, point out a line for putting, but in so doing the putting green shall not be touched (see Figure 3-2). No mark shall be placed anywhere to indicate a line for putting.

(The penalty for breach of the rule is loss of hole in match play and two strokes in stroke play.)

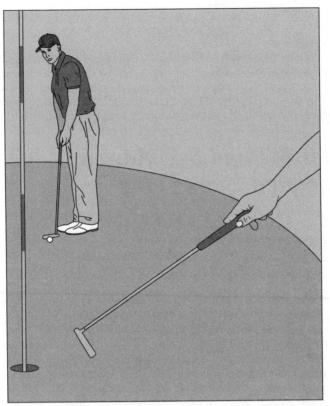

Figure 3-2: Your caddie may point out a line to putt, but the green may not be touched.

Rule 13-1: Ball Played as It Lies

The ball shall be played as it lies (see Figure 3-3), except as otherwise provided in the rules.

Rules 16-1 and 16-2: The Putting Green

16-1 — General

16-1a — Touching Line of Putt: The line of put must not be touched except:

(i) the player may move sand and loose soil on the putting green and other loose impediments by picking them up and brushing them aside with his hand or a club without pressing anything down.

(ii) in addressing the ball, the player may place the club in front of the ball without pressing anything down.

Figure 3-3: Even though this isn't a great lie, the player still has to play the ball, unless indicated otherwise in the rules.

(iii) in measuring — Rule 10-4

(iv) in lifting the ball — Rule 16-b

(v) in pressing down a ball marker

(vi) in repairing old hole plugs or ball marks on the putting green — Rule 16-1c (see Figure 3-4)

(vii) in removing movable obstructions

(The one thing missing here is spike marks left by golf shoes, and you may not fix them.)

16-1b — Lifting Ball: A ball on the putting green may be lifted and, if desired, cleaned. A ball so lifted shall be replaced on the spot from which it was lifted.

16-1c — Repair of Hole Plugs, Ball Marks, and Other Damage: The player may repair an old hole plug or damage to the putting green caused by the impact of the ball, whether or not the player's ball lies on the putting green. If a ball or ball-marker is accidentally moved in the process of such repair, the ball or ball-marker shall be replaced, without penalty. Any other damage to the putting green shall not be repaired as it might assist the player in his subsequent play of the hole.

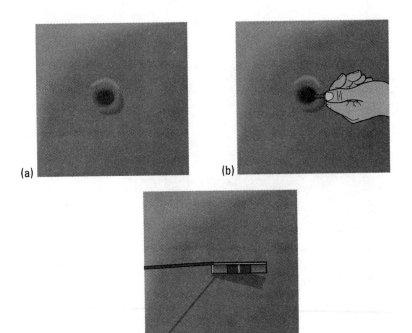

(a)

(b)

(c)

Figure 3-4: You may touch the line of putt to repair a ball mark on the green.

16-1d — Testing Surface: During the play of a hole, a player shall not test the surface of the putting green by rolling a ball or roughening or scraping the surface.

16-1e — Standing Astride or on Line of Putt: The player shall not make a stroke on the putting green from a stance astride, or with either foot touching, the line of putt or an extension of that line behind the ball.

16-1f — Playing Stroke While Another Ball in Motion: The player shall not play a stroke while another ball is in motion after a stroke from the putting green, except that, if a player does so, he incurs no penalty if it was his turn to play.

(The penalty for breach of Rule 16-1 is loss of hole for match play and two strokes for stroke play.)

16-2 — Ball Overhanging Hole: When any part of the ball overhangs the lip of the hole, the player is allowed enough time to reach the hole without unreasonable delay and an additional ten seconds to determine whether the ball is at rest. If by then the ball has not fallen into the hole, it is deemed to be at rest. If the ball subsequently falls into the hole, the player is deemed to have holed out with his last stroke, and he shall add a penalty stroke to his score for the hole; otherwise there is no penalty under this rule.

Rules 17-1 and 17-3: The Flagstick

17-1 — Flagstick Attended, Removed, or Held Up: Before and during the stroke, the player may have the flagstick attended, removed or held up to indicate the position of the hole. This may be done only on the authority of the player before he plays his stroke.

If, prior to the stroke, the flagstick is attended, removed or held up by anyone with the player's knowledge and no objection is made, the player shall be deemed to have authorized it. If anyone attends or holds up the flagstick or stands near the hole while a stroke is being played, he shall be deemed to be attending the flagstick until the ball comes to rest.

17-3 — Ball Striking Flagstick or Attendant: The players' ball shall not strike:

17-3a: The flagstick when attended, removed or held up by the player, his partner or either of their caddies, or by another person with the player's authority or prior knowledge; or

17-3b: The player's caddie, his partner or his partner's caddie when attending the flagstick, or another person attending the flagstick with the player's authority or prior knowledge or anything carried by any such person; or

17-3c: The flagstick in the hole, unattended, when the ball has been played from the putting green.

(The penalty for breach of Rule 17-3 in match play is loss of hole, and in stroke play, two strokes and the ball shall be played as it lies.)

Rule 23: Loose Impediments

23-1 — Relief: Except when both the loose impediment and the ball lie in or touch the same hazard, any loose impediment may be moved without penalty (see Figure 3-5). If the ball moves, see Rule 18-2c. (That rule states that a player should incur a penalty stroke if the ball moves after any loose impediment within a club length has been touched by a player, his partner or either of their caddies off the green. There is no penalty if it moves during such removal on the green; the ball simply needs to be replaced.)

When a ball is in motion, a loose impediment which might influence the movement of the ball shall not be removed.

Figure 3-5: You may move loose impediments such as leaves from around your ball without penalty except when the ball and the loose impediment lie in or touch the same hazard.

Rules 24-1 and 24-2: Obstructions, Movable and Immovable

24-1 — Movable Obstructions: A player may obtain relief from a movable obstruction as follows:

24-1a: If the ball does not lie in or on the obstruction, the obstruction may be removed. If the ball moves, it shall be replaced, and there is no penalty provided that the movement of the ball is directly attributable to the removal of the obstruction.

24-1b: If the ball lies in or on the obstruction, the ball may be lifted, without penalty, and the obstruction removed. The ball shall through the green or in a hazard be dropped, or on the putting green be placed, as near as possible to the spot directly under the place where the ball lay in or on the obstruction, but not nearer the hole.

The ball may be cleaned when lifted under Rule 24-1.

When a ball is in motion, an obstruction which might influence the movement of the ball, other than the attended flagstick or equipment of the players, shall not be removed.

Note: If a ball to be dropped or placed under this rule is not immediately recoverable, another ball may be substituted.

24-2 — Immovable Obstruction

24-2a — Interference: Interference by an immovable obstruction occurs when a ball lies in or on the obstruction, or so close to the obstruction that the obstruction interferes with the player's stance or the area of his intended swing. If the player's ball lies on the putting green, interference also occurs if an immovable obstruction on the putting green intervenes on his line of putt. Otherwise, intervention on the line of play is not, of itself, interference under this rule.

24-2b — Relief: Except when the ball is in a water hazard or a lateral water hazard, a player may obtain relief from interference by an immovable obstruction, without penalty, as follows:

(i) Through the Green: If the ball lies through the green, the nearest point of relief shall be determined which is not in a hazard or on the putting green. The player shall lift the ball and drop it within one club-length of and not nearer the hole than the nearest point of relief on a part of the course which avoids interference (as defined) by the immovable obstruction and is not in a hazard or on a putting green (see Figure 3-6).

(ii) In a Bunker: If the ball is in a bunker, the player shall lift and drop the ball in accordance with Clause (i) above, except that the nearest point of relief must be in the bunker and the ball must be dropped in the bunker.

(iii) On the Putting Green: If the ball lies on the putting green, the player shall lift the ball and place it at the nearest point of relief which is not in the hazard. The nearest point of relief may be off the putting green.

The ball may be cleaned when lifted under Rule 24-2b.

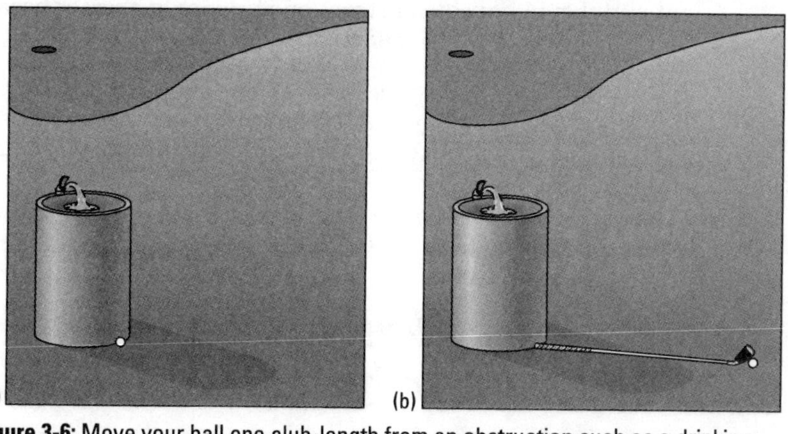

(a)   (b)

Figure 3-6: Move your ball one club-length from an obstruction such as a drinking fountain, but no closer to the hole than where you originally hit it.

Exception: A player may not obtain relief under Rule 24-2b if (a) it is clearly unreasonable for him to play a stroke because of interference by anything other than an immovable construction or (b) interference by an immovable obstruction would occur only through use of an unnecessarily abnormal stance, swing or direction of play.

Note 1: If a ball is in a water hazard (including a lateral water hazard), the player is not entitled to relief without penalty from interference by an immovable obstruction. The player shall play the ball as it lies or proceed under Rule 26-1.

Note 2: If a ball to be dropped or placed under this rule is not immediately recoverable, another ball may be substituted.

24-2c — Ball Lost: It is a question of fact whether a ball lost after having been struck toward an immovable obstruction is lost in the obstruction. In order to treat the ball as lost in the obstruction, there must be reasonable evidence to that effect. In the absence of such evidence, the ball must be treated as a lost ball and Rule 27 applies.

If the ball is lost in an immovable obstruction, the spot where the ball last entered the obstruction shall be determined and, for the purpose of applying this rule, the ball shall be deemed to lie at this spot.

(i) Through the Green: If the ball last entered the immovable obstruction at a spot through the green, the player may substitute another ball without penalty and take relief as prescribed in Rule 24-2b(i).

(ii) In a Bunker: If the ball last entered the immovable obstruction at a spot in a bunker, the player may substitute another ball without penalty and take relief as prescribed in Rule 24-2b(ii).

(iii) In a Water Hazard (including a lateral water hazard): If the ball last entered the immovable obstruction at a spot in a water hazard, the player is not entitled to relief without penalty.

(iv) On the Putting Green: If the ball entered the immovable obstruction at a spot on the putting green, the player may substitute another ball without penalty and take relief as prescribed in Rule 24-2b(iii).

(The penalty for breach of rule is loss of hole in match play and two strokes in stroke play.)

Rule 26-1: Water Hazards — Ball in Water Hazard

It is a question of fact whether a ball lost after having been struck toward a water hazard is lost inside or outside the hazard. In order to treat the ball as lost in the hazard, there must be reasonable evidence that the ball lodged in it. In the absence of such evidence, the ball must be treated as a lost ball and Rule 27 applies.

If a ball is in or is lost in a water hazard (whether the ball lies in water or not), the player may under penalty of one stroke:

26-1a: Play a ball as nearly as possible at the spot from which the original ball was last played (see Rule 20-5); or

26-1b: Drop a ball behind the water hazard, keeping the point at which the original ball last crossed the margin of the water hazard directly between the hole and the spot on which the ball is dropped, with no limit to how far behind the water hazard and the ball may be dropped (see Figure 3-7); or

26-1c: As additional options available only if the ball last crossed the margin of a lateral water hazard, drop the ball outside the water hazard within two club lengths of and not nearer the hole than (i) the point where the original ball last crossed the margin of the water hazard, or (ii) a point on the opposite margin of the water hazard equidistant from the hole.

The ball may be cleaned when lifted under this rule.

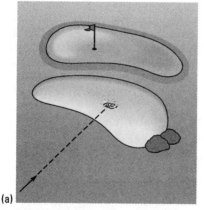 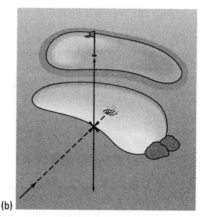

(a)   (b)

Figure 3-7: Water, water, everywhere . . .

Rules 27-1 and 27-2: Ball Lost or Out of Bounds; Provisional Ball

27-1 — Ball Lost or Out of Bounds: If a ball is lost or is out of bounds, the player shall play a ball, under penalty of one stroke, as nearly as possible as the spot from which the original ball was last played (see Rule 20-5).

Exceptions:

1) If there is reasonable evidence that the original ball is lost in a water hazard, the player shall proceed in accordance with Rule 26-1.

2) If there is reasonable evidence that the original ball is lost in an immovable obstruction (Rule 24-2c) or an abnormal ground condition (Rule 25-1c) the player may proceed under the applicable rule.

(The penalty for breach of Rule 27-1 is, as usual, loss of hole in match play and two strokes in stroke play.)

27-2 — Provisional Ball

27-2a — Procedure: If a ball may be lost outside a water hazard or may be out of bounds, to save time a player may play another ball provisionally in accordance with Rule 27-1. The player shall inform his opponent in match play or his marker or a fellow-competitor in stroke play that he intends to play a provisional ball, and he shall play it before he or his partner goes forward to search for the original ball.

If he fails to do so and plays another ball, such ball is not a provisional ball and becomes the ball in play under penalty of stroke and distance (Rule 27-1); the original ball is deemed to be lost.

27-2b — When Provisional Ball Becomes Ball in Play: The player may play a provisional ball until he reaches the place where the original ball is likely to be. If he plays a stroke with the provisional ball from the place where the original ball is likely to be or from a point nearer the hole than that place, the original ball is deemed to be lost and the provisional ball becomes the ball in play under penalty of stroke and distance.

If the original ball is lost outside a water hazard or is out of bounds, the provisional becomes the ball in play, under penalty of stroke and distance.

If there is reasonable evidence that the original ball is not lost in a water hazard, the player shall proceed in accordance with Rule 26-1.

Exception: If there is reasonable evidence that the original ball is lost in an immovable obstruction (Rule 24-2c) or an abnormal ground condition (Rule 25-1c), the player may proceed under the applicable rule.

27-2c — When Provisional Ball to be Abandoned: If the original ball is neither lost nor out of bounds, the player shall abandon the provisional ball and continue play with the original ball. If he fails to do so, any further strokes played with the provisional shall constitute playing a wrong ball and the provisions of Rule 15 shall apply.

ANECDOTE

Willie Nelson's Right Rules for Golfing

Down in Spicewood, Texas, is a 9-hole, public golf course called Pedernales that is laid out on 76 acres of land in the hill country about 30 miles outside Austin. The par-36 track measures some 3,300 yards and is named after a local river. It is also owned by musician and songwriter Willie Nelson.

"In fact," Nelson chuckles, "I have owned it twice. I originally bought it in 1976 and then lost it to the Internal Revenue Service for a while in 1991 when I was going through all my tax trouble. But some friends of mine bought it from the government and then held it for me until I could buy it back from them."

An 18-handicapper who has been known to play as many as 100 holes in a single day, Willie is a man with a passion for golf and a sense of humor about the sport. He thinks the game should be fun and likes to keep things light around his course, which is used mostly by local duffers. So he has created his own set of rules and regulations that he expects players to follow at Pedernales, which is about half a mile away from Nelson's home and next door to a recording studio. And he makes sure they are posted on a bulletin board outside the pro shop. They are:

- No bikinis, miniskirts, or sexually explicit attire is allowed on anyone except women.

- There is no such thing as a lost ball because sooner or later someone will find it and put it back in play.

- There is no such thing as a lipped ball because the laws of gravity outweigh the laws of golf, and the ball will eventually go into the hole.

- Gambling is forbidden unless you are stuck and need a legal deduction for charitable or educational expenses.

- When another is shooting, no one should talk, whistle, hum, clink change, or pass gas.

- Please replace divots, repair ball marks, smooth bunkers, and have the office tell your spouse you are in conference.

Those aren't your everyday rules of golf (and it is highly unlikely that the USGA would ever ask Willie to sit on its executive committee). But as Nelson is quick to point out, when you own your own course, you can make things up as you go along.

Rule 28: Ball Unplayable

The player shall declare his ball unplayable at any place on the course except when the ball is in a water hazard. The player is the sole judge as to whether his ball is unplayable.

If a player deems his ball to be unplayable, he shall, under penalty of one stroke:

28a: Play a ball as nearly as possible to the spot from which the original ball was last played; or

28b: Drop a ball within two club lengths of the spot where the ball lay but not nearer the hole (see Figure 3-8); or

28c: Drop a ball behind the point where the ball lay, keeping that point directly between the hole and the spot on which the ball is dropped, with no limit to how far behind that point the ball may be dropped.

If the unplayable ball is in a bunker, the player may proceed under Clause a, b, or c. If he elects to proceed under Clause b or c, a ball must be dropped in the bunker.

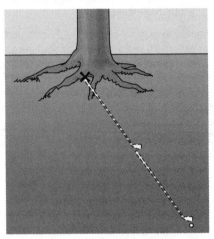

Figure 3-8: If your ball is unplayable, you can move it two club lengths away from the spot where the ball lay, as long as you don't move it any closer to the hole, but you have to take a one-stroke penalty.

How the Rules Have Been Interpreted

The Official Rules of Golf tells you all about the regulations that govern the game. But it doesn't shed much light on the different ways they have been interpreted over the years. And those of us who have smacked a 5-iron or flopped a wedge have stories about the different ways the rules of golf have been applied when we have played. Plenty of stories. In addition, we've seen what has happened to the touring professionals who tee it up on TV every week. Some of the rules and their interpretations make perfect sense; others are maddeningly inane; most are devastating; and they all have some educational value for those of us who like the game.

If people ever decided to write songs about golf penalties, the tunes would be as sad and as gut-wrenching as a Country & Western ballad.

The outcomes around the greens and fairways can often be as tough as those nasty trailer-park breakups in which the wife leaves her husband with the kids in the pickup, empties out his bank account, and then sics the dog on him.

Do it once more, with feeling

The scene is the 2000 Solheim Cup match between women teams from the U.S. and Europe, and on the 13th hole of the Loch Lomond course in Scotland, Sweden's Anika Sorenstam chips a ball from just off the green into the hole for what appears to be a win and a chance to go only one-down to the American duo of Kelly Robbins and Pat Hurst.

But as Sorenstam and her partner Janice Moodie start jumping up and down, Robbins senses that something is amiss and realizes that Sorenstam had played out of turn; it was Robbins who technically was away. Robbins tells the match referee Barbara Trammel about the problem, and after she paces off the differences in distance between Sorenstam's and Robbins's balls, she determines that the Swedish player was indeed a yard and a half closer.

Under Rule 10-1c, the U.S. had the right to ask Sorenstam to replay the shot, and after consulting with captain Pat Bradley, that's exactly what the squad did, much to the European's dismay. Sorenstam tried to work her magic again, but to no avail, and the second ball made it onto the green but went nowhere near the cup. The American ended up winning the hole and ultimately the match. And Sorenstam was reduced to tears and spoke harshly of the incident: "It makes you ask the question: What would have happened if I did not make it?" she asked. "Who knows what the turnout of the match would have been. A lot of things could be different right now."

The Europeans ended up winning the Solheim Cup, so that match with the replayed chip really didn't matter in the scheme of things. But it upset quite a few of the players, and that's too bad. For as unfair as that rule may be in some people's eyes, it is still a rule, and the Americans really had no choice but to ask for that second chip. It was their right and their duty.

I am a rock

In January 1999, Tiger Woods came upon an interesting situation when he played the 13th hole at the Phoenix Open and watched an errant tee shot come to rest behind a large boulder. (What is it about 13th holes?) When Woods asked PGA Tour rules official Orlando Pope if the boulder was a "loose impediment" and therefore movable under Rule 23-1, Pope said that so long as play wasn't disrupted, Woods could move the boulder. This was, in the true meaning of the word, a boulder, and not even Tiger Woods could so much as roll it by himself. But a dozen members of the gallery volunteered to help out, and they were able to roll the rock right out of the way. Woods went on to make birdie on the hole and ended up third for the event, behind Rococo Mediate and Justin Leonard.

Say again

I was playing a match at my club one day, and an elderly gentleman who was giving me a true run for my money kept asking what club I hit after my approach shots and drives to par-3s. I was not aware of it at the time, but that was a violation of the rule (8-1) that prohibits opponents from giving and/or asking for advice from each other. So I kept telling him what I hit, out of sheer naiveté and a sense of false manners. And he kept going to town on what I was saying. So after I hit a 4-iron into a 180-yard par-3 green, I received the usual inquiry, and said, "6-iron." Frankly, I could barely contain myself when I watched him ask for that same club from his caddie and then leave his shot about 40 yards from the front of the green. And I did all I could do to keep from laughing as he wondered why he had come up short. Though he didn't know it, he had listened to me one too many times.

"What a stupid I am!"

There is no more tragic tale about golf and the rules than the one about Argentinean golfer Roberto de Vicenzo. Having won the British Open the year before, he came to the 1968 Masters as one of the favorites. And after he shot 65 on the final round, it looked as if he was going to win. His playing partner Bob Goalby was also having a good round, and he ended up tying de Vincenzo for the lead. It looked like a playoff was going to take place the next day.

But then the wheels came completely off. A check of de Vincenzo's scorecard showed that a "4" and not a "3" had been recorded at the 17th hole, and with that mistake, his score actually added up to 66, not 65. De Vincenzo had signed the card, and even though it was his playing partner, Bob Goalby, who had originally written down the wrong number, it was up to de Vincenzo to check the score before he attested to it. If the score recorded was lower than that actually taken by the golfer, he would have been disqualified. Because the recorded score was actually higher, he simply had to live with the number. But his 66 meant that he would finished one stroke back in second place. No playoff. No green jacket. No immortality. "What a stupid I am," de Vincenzo said after his mistake was revealed. And it was something that would dog him the rest of his life.

Make golf, not war

Not a lot of people played golf in Great Britain during World War II, and for good reasons, what with bombs falling from Luftwaffe planes, German U-boats sneaking along the coast and Nazi invasion forces massing across the Channel. But for those who could get out to the course — and who were brave enough to try — there were certain "conditions" drawn up specifically for those times by Major G.L. Edsell, Secretary of St. Mellons Golf and Country Club. In time, they were adopted by most of the golfing populace in the U.K. And clearly, the game had never before — and has never since — been governed by such a code. It was as follows:

1. Players are asked to collect bomb and shell splinters from the fairways to save these causing damage to the mowers.

2. In competitions, during gunfire or while bombs are falling, players may take cover without penalty for ceasing play.

3. The positions of known delayed-action bombs are marked by red and white flags placed at reasonably, but not guaranteed, safe distances from the bombs.

4. Shell and/or bomb splinters on the greens may be removed without penalty. On the fairways or in bunkers within a club's length of a ball they may be moved without penalty and no penalty shall be incurred if a ball is thereby caused to move accidentally.

5. A ball moved by enemy action may be replaced as near as possible to where it lay, or if lost and destroyed a ball may be dropped not nearer the hole without penalty.

6. A ball lying in any crater may be lifted and dropped not nearer the hole preserving the line to the hole, without penalty.

7. A player whose stroke is affected by the simultaneous explosion of a bomb or shell, or by machine gun fire, may play another ball from the same place. Penalty one stroke.

You have to admire the author of these makeshift rules for figuring out a way for players to enjoy golf during one of the darkest times in British history. And you have to admit, they seem about as sensible as they are funny. But a one-stroke penalty for replacing a ball that was destroyed by a bomb or machine fire? That is definitely more than a little harsh. And it's a good thing that players were able to run for cover during an air raid without fear of being penalized, because that is just what I would be worrying about as I was dodging bombs.

Part II
The Unwritten Rules: How to Handle Yourself on (And off) the Course

The 5th Wave   By Rich Tennant

"Remember, it's not proper etiquette to immediately talk business on a golf outing. Wait until at least the 6th hole to bring up the pool toy account."

In this part . . .

*I*n the chapters in this part, you'll get the lowdown on the etiquette surrounding the game of golf, on and off the course. I cover everything from the differences between public and private courses, to how to handle yourself on the driving range and putting green. Finally, because golf has become a very important part of business for many people, I give you some special rules to keep in mind when there's more at stake than your score.

Chapter 4

Universal Truths and Other Rules to Live By

. . . .

In This Chapter

▶ Knowing the basics of good golf etiquette

▶ Playing in tournaments with ease

▶ Using the handicap system with the proper etiquette

▶ Playing with caddies

▶ Tipping with the best of them

. . . .

*T*o some people, the topic of golf etiquette seems about as huge as quantum physics. Although nowhere near as complicated as the Theory of Relativity, the game of golf has many nuances that extend far beyond the actual rules of play, and knowing as much about them as you can is important. Don't worry, no one expects you to have an ency-clopedic knowledge of golf etiquette after only a few years in the game. Picking up all the relevant do's and don'ts takes a lot of time — and a lot of rounds. Even the most experienced players find that they learn new things about manners and behavior on the golf course all the time. I know I do, and I've been playing for some 30 years.

What's important, then, is not so much a complete and total compre-hension of golf etiquette but rather a respect for what is and isn't acceptable, a willingness to learn as much as you can about those unwritten rules, and a basic common sensibility when it comes to play-ing the game and deciding what is — and isn't — right to do.

In this chapter, I introduce you to the world of golf etiquette and let you know how to carry yourself on a course with ease. I begin with the basics — a list of dos and don'ts for the game of golf, no matter where you're playing or with whom. Then I move on to the specifics, like play-ing in tournaments, using the handicap system, and using caddies.

Golf Etiquette 101: The Basics

Just like etiquette in other areas of your life, etiquette in the game of golf is really just about knowing the rules that govern behavior and following them. Knowing why a rule is in place isn't as important as just making sure you obey it — at least when it comes to etiquette. So here's a list of do's and don'ts for the game of golf. If you know nothing else about golf etiquette, make sure you are at least familiar with the following:

- **Don't talk after a person has addressed his ball.** Golf requires a lot of concentration, and disturbing any player with chatter as he is getting ready to hit is rude.

- **Make sure the group in front of you is well out of range before you hit your shot.** Few things are more aggravating than some yahoo crunching a 3-wood onto a green that you're still occupying and then trying to excuse it (and the ball that has just bounced off your leg) by saying, "I'm sorry, I just hit my career shot. I had no idea it would go so far." Have better sense than that — and better manners. If there's any chance you may be able to hit someone in front of you, don't take the swing — or the risk.

- **Yell "Fore!" — quickly and loudly — if it looks like you may hit someone with your ball.** Any chance you can give someone to protect himself is appreciated. (And try not to laugh too hard at the reactions some players have when they hear that word. I've watched people hit the deck as though they were dodging a cruise missile, tap dance around like Gregory Hines, run for daylight like Walter Payton, or freeze like a Popsicle. It can be very amusing.)

- **Help out the course superintendent by replacing all your divots, raking the bunkers, and fixing the ball marks on the green.** And don't be shy about picking up after others. Although that isn't technically your responsibility, conscientious golfers take care of a divot or ball mark that someone else has left behind. The credo to live by is this: Leave the course in better shape than you found it.

- **Help the superintendent and his workers by making sure they are out of the way when you hit (or are at least aware that you are hitting into them).** I've watched people at my club pound approach shots into greens while guys are still mowing the grass. And they don't even try to alert them. Show those workers the same courtesy you show others, and make sure they know the balls are coming.

- **Always be sure that the person in your group who is farthest from the hole is allowed to hit first.**

- **Don't walk way ahead of the group while someone is hitting (or getting ready to hit).** Peeling off to the sides to find and then hit your own ball is acceptable. In fact, that is *de rigeur* for golfers who want to maintain a reasonable pace of play (by being ready to hit when it is their turn). But everyone should be roughly the same distance from the hole. If you wander up ahead of everyone, that can be distracting for the rest of your group — and also unsafe.

✔ **Don't take too many practice swings before a shot.** Two should be the maximum. This keeps the game moving at a comfortable pace.

✔ **Don't prowl around the green for five minutes trying to line up your putts and discern every undulation.** Take a look at what you have before you, and then make the shot. Just because the pros take forever around the green doesn't mean *you* have to.

✔ **Be ready to hit when it's your turn.** I always try to mark off my yardage to the hole while I am on the way to my ball and make my club selection while my partner or opponent is in the process of hitting. Obviously, I don't pull clubs out of my bag while my partner is in the middle of his back swing. But I do try to accomplish as much as possible as far as shot preparation is concerned so I'm ready to go when it's my turn.

✔ **Line up your putt while others are doing the same, so when it is your turn to make a run at the hole, you are ready.**

✔ **Don't tell stories at the expense of holding up the group.** Stop your tale when it is time for you — or others — to play your ball, and then pick up your story later. There is no reason for you to keep people standing around the fairway listening to your story while others are waiting to play.

✔ **Keep up with the group in front of you.** That really is your best gauge of pace of play. As long as the group in front of you is no more than a hole ahead, you're doing fine.

✔ **If you can't keep up with the group in front of you, let the folks behind you play through.** Stand aside, preferably on the tee or green, and allow them to hit their shots and move ahead. Some people consider allowing others to play through to be a completely humiliating experience, and they would rather you run 1,000 volts of electricity through their system than give up their place on the golf course. But there really is no other option for slow players. And if you keep a proper pace, you should never have to do that in the first place.

Note: Single players really have no standing on a golf course, especially if they go out at peak times. So don't expect to fly through group after group if you are solo. Doing so is not only disruptive, it's also rude. Twosomes are only moderately more acceptable in that regard, and most times they should be allowed to play through slower and larger groups. But I have no sympathy for the pair that goes out on a Saturday or Sunday morning and tries to force their way around at primetime.

My advice is simple: If you want to play as a single, be among the first or last ones out on a given day and don't feel it is your right to bull your way through the course. And if you want to play with a friend as a twosome, try to get an early start as well and play at the less crowded times so you cause the least amount of chaos for other golfers.

- ✔ **Keep your round of golf to four hours or less.** I have played 18 holes in less than three hours on plenty of occasions, without rushing. I know, avoiding the monster round at busy public courses is difficult. But golf really should not be an all-day affair.

- ✔ **Don't walk across someone's putting line on the green.** If you do, you can give him what my friends and I call a *bigfoot,* and that could affect the direction and speed of her putt. Walking across someone else's putting line is less of a problem than it used to be, because most players these days wear soft-spiked golf shoes. But it is still a no-no.

- ✔ **Walk off the green as soon as you're finished putting.** That, too, will speed up play and allow anyone behind you to play up promptly. Technically, you should also wait until you get off the green to mark your scorecard, again in the interest of fast play. But I often mark people's scores as they putt, and after I am done. That way, I'm not lingering around the green with pencil in hand when everyone else is gone. It's fine to do it that way so long as you move on with the rest of your group and free up the green immediately.

- ✔ **Pick up any broken tees you leave — or find — on the teeing area.** It will help out the superintendent and his crew and not only make the tee look better but also protect the mowers when the grass is cut.

- ✔ **Never leave your tee in the ground after you have hit.** Tees left in the ground can be rough on the mower and be a real pain to other players who have to dig the tee out before they hit. Never, ever pound your tee into the ground with your club after a bad shot (or after a good shot, for that matter). It's bad sportsmanship — and besides, someone's going to have to pull it out.

- ✔ **Don't lean on your putter while on the green.** That can leave a divot in the ground that may damage the green and affect the roll of someone else's ball.

- ✔ **Don't stand behind someone as they hit their putt.** Some people like to do this to get a good read of the line, but it is very bad form. Unless, of course, it is your partner putting in a match, and he allows you to do that as his teammate.

- ✔ **Walk whenever possible.** And if you must play in a cart, keep it away from the greens, tees, and bunkers.

- ✔ **Keep an extra ball or two in your pants pocket so you can reload quickly if you need to hit a second shot or a provisional.** Anything to save time and ensure a faster round, right?

✔ **Keep an eye on where the balls of your partner and opponents go.** You can help maintain a good pace of play by knowing exactly where to look for errant shots. And many eyes means less work for all involved.

✔ **Keep in mind that you have only five minutes to look for a ball before it is declared lost.** And as far as I'm concerned, you should cut that time down to three minutes if there are people waiting to play behind you.

✔ **Play only one ball while on the course and leave the practicing for the driving range.**

✔ **Don't litter, and pick up after people who do.**

✔ **Don't drag your feet on the green.** Even if you aren't wearing metal spikes, you can damage the green that way and mar the putting surface.

✔ **Respect the employees of the course you're playing.** Treat them well.

✔ **Always check in with the pro shop before you go out on any course.** Courses want to keep records of who is playing, and it gives them a chance to tell you about specific problems or issues of which you need to be aware.

✔ **Always listen to what the pro says.** He is the one in charge of the golf program, and his word should be heeded. If he tells you to go off the back nine instead of the front, go off the back. If he tells you that you can't, don't. A good pro knows how to manage a golf course and understand what's what. He knows it better than most of his members, and he deserves their undivided attention and respect.

✔ **Refrain from giving "lessons" to other members of your foursome when you are out on the course.** Doing so is obnoxious and holds up play. Offer tips only if asked. (And the best tip may be: "Go see a real golf pro.")

✔ **Know the rules.** Read the USGA's *Official Rules of Golf*.

✔ **Watch where you swing your clubs.** Make sure you don't inadvertently clock someone on the head.

✔ **Be careful where you stand while others are hitting their shots.** To the side of a player is not only safe but unobtrusive. Never stand behind someone's ball, even if you are out of range of his swing. That can be terribly distracting to the person making the shot.

✔ **Do not throw your clubs.** It is bad manners, it can upset your playing partners and it can be dangerous to your fellow golfers.

✔ **A mulligan is fine on the first hole if everybody in your group agrees (and if you treat it on your scorecard the way the Official Rules of Golf say you should).** But take only one. Some folks like to "hit 'til they're happy," but that just holds everyone up.

✔ **Establish the bet for the day, if any, on the first tee and make sure all aspects are agreed upon before you head off.** You don't want someone trying to change things up partway through the round. Especially if you're beating them up.

✔ **Keep in mind that a little verbal abuse of your playing partners and opponents is well within the realm of good golf course decorum.** But go easy on bosses, coworkers, and people you don't know very well. Feel free, however, to be a little rougher on those childhood friends you play with every week. Ask the broker in your group about that lemon stock he sold you a few years ago. Tell the magazine publisher how much you like his competitor's most recent issue. Inquire as to whether your opponent has been able to cure his incessant snap-hook just as he gets ready to tee off. Or whether his ex-wife has started dating anyone yet. After all, this game is supposed to be fun, and if you can't take a little heat. . . .

✔ **Keep your complaints to a minimum.** We're all pretty lucky to be able to go out and play golf, and no one really wants to hear a lot of whining about everything you perceive to be wrong with the course or the club you're playing. Sadly, more and more people seem to be complaining these days, demanding greater services — and perfection — from their golf clubs than at any other time in memory. That's too bad, because the gripes are not only ridiculous most of the time, but they also cause enormous grief for the people running the course or club and make it tougher for the players who have to listen to that nonsense to enjoy their day. I have heard guys rail about there being too many leaves on the greens — during a late fall day in New England. I have listened to mental shut-ins go crazy over a few geese who leave droppings on the fairways on a coastal Connecticut course, with some going so far as to attack the geese with golf clubs and insisting that clubs waste thousands of dollars a year on dogs that are supposed to chase the geese away. If something really is wrong with the course you're playing, bring it to the manager's or pro's attention. Otherwise, be thankful for what you have and keep quiet.

✔ **Be humble. Be respectful. Be on your best behavior.** I know too many people now who strut around with the most remarkable arrogance and attitude, all because they have made a few bucks on the stock market and think that they can do no wrong. They berate caddies and pro shop workers. They refuse to follow the rules. They act loudly and like to show off. Bad ideas, one and all. No one needs to act that way, and no one in their right mind wants to be around people who do. That sort of behavior has no place anywhere, especially not in the game of golf.

Playing in Tournaments

To enjoy tournament golf you don't have to be a scratch player with a deadly draw and a strong putting stroke. Men and women of all ages and abilities can enter tournaments at clubs or facilities, play with people of their same level, and have a fantastic time going at it on the links. If you like sports, and like competing at them, then nothing can be quite so much fun.

But there are important things to keep in mind, etiquette-wise, when you play events. (You knew I was getting to this, didn't you?) I recommend that you consider the following do's and don'ts as you get ready to win your silver:

✔ **Always shake hands at the start of a match and wish the other player or team good luck.** I know that being nice to the person, or persons, you are about to do battle with is sometimes difficult, especially if they're folks you don't particularly care for. But get over it. Respectful gestures like a handshake set a good tone for the match. And frankly, they're the right thing to do.

✔ **Show up on time.** You are disqualified from most tournaments if you miss your tee time. And even if you are allowed the latitude to continue competing despite your tardiness, you're not off the hook. In all likelihood, you will have upset your playing partner and opponents by being late. And you just may cause a rift that will linger throughout the round and make it much less enjoyable than it otherwise could have been.

✔ **Acknowledge a well-played shot.** You don't have to give your opponent a high five, but a laconic "Good shot" or even a smile and a nod is an appropriate and sportsmanlike response to a solid hit. At the same time, don't patronize your opponent with false praise when he has hit a bad or mediocre ball. He doesn't want to hear that from you, and he shouldn't have to.

ANECDOTE

With friends like these. . . .

Two friends of mine, George Rippey and Craig Atkinson, waited 90 minutes for one of their opponents to show up for a simple match-play event. The guy they were playing against had been arrested for driving while intoxicated the evening before and had spent the night in jail. His excuse may have been legitimate, but it steamed Craig to no end, especially after the newly-released jailbird asked, with tongue only slightly in cheek, if he could go down to the range and hit a few balls before they started. So it surprised no one that Craig, whom we long ago nicknamed "Crazy" for his precariously fragile mental state during athletic events, proceeded to hit two grounders off the first tee and come as close as is humanly possible to actually exploding.

There is no reason ever to put people through something like that. Even if you've spent the night in jail.

✔ **Stand in the right place when the other player is hitting.** That is usually to one side of a golfer as he addresses his ball, either in front of him, or in back. And stay still. Also, don't be afraid to ask a player to move, or refrain from moving, if he is bothering you with his position while you're trying to hit the ball.

✔ **Play at a reasonable pace.** I'm all for fast play, but the fact is, tournaments take a bit longer than your regular recreational rounds because more is generally at stake. Still, you don't have to line up a putt from ten different angles or take five practice swings for each shot. Concentrate hard, think about your strokes, but keep moving.

✔ **Drop the running commentary.** I know people who like to give you a full recap of every shot, from address to follow-through, and all the things that went wrong in the process. I'm sorry, but I really don't care, especially if I'm playing a match. Making remarks that may influence your opponent's decision-making when it comes his time to hit (for example, commenting on the speed and grain of the green or perhaps the direction of the wind) is distracting. Keep those thoughts to yourself. If you have to vent, do so with your playing partner or caddie, not with your opponents.

✔ **Don't lash out.** Okay, so you've been playing horribly and having terrible luck in the process. Part of you wants to throw your club into the lake, yet another part knows that behaving that way is very bad form and something that could really disturb your opponent. Resist the impulse to lash out. Take a deep breath. Count to ten. Do whatever it takes to control your frustration.

My just dessert

I remember playing a match some years ago against my friend Nat Foote. I was down three holes after six. Plain and simple, he was stomping me. On the 7th hole, I had a fairly easy chip, but I skulled it, and the ball went screaming over the green and into the back bunker.

I was so furious that I quickly hurled my club in that general direction, despite the pre-chuck protestations of Nat, who had seen me wind up like an Olympic hammer thrower. He clearly found my actions upsetting and let me back into the match by 3-putting the hole and allowing me to tie him with a bogey. And then he topped his drive on the next tee and ended up losing that hole as well.

At that point, I felt terrible, in part because I was playing badly, in part because I had lost my cool, but mostly because my display of pique had affected Nat's game. It was the only time I ever wanted to lose a match on a golf course. I certainly didn't deserve to win after what I had done, and Nat didn't deserve to lose after what I had done to him. Fortunately, he pulled himself together quickly enough to maintain his lead and send me packing, which is exactly what I deserved.

Great outbursts in golf tournament history

I know, I shouldn't be glorifying boorish behavior. But I find it hard not to relate a couple of humorous tales involving golfers who simply couldn't take it any more.

Like the guy playing in the big member-guest tournament at our golf club one year. He got so frustrated with his game that he threw his entire bag, clubs and all, into a water hazard we call the lagoon. It took about five minutes for the bag and all its rather expensive contents, to sink to the bottom, and I'm told the entire group, which included four golfers and a pair of caddies, stood there silently and watched it go down like the Titanic.

And then there are those great Tommy Bolt stories. Tommy Bolt, for the uninitiated, is a longtime PGA Tour player and the winner of the 1958 U.S. Open. He is also a man famous for breaking a club or two in his day. One story has the golfer asking his caddie for his 6-iron during a particularly brutal round. "I'm sorry, Mr. Bolt," the man replied. "We're down to your 3, 7, and 9." And that's because Tommy had already snapped all the others in half.

Award-winning writer Dan Jenkins once told me about a row he got into with Bolt over a story in which Dan reported about the golfer breaking his 5-iron during a tournament. Bolt confronted Jenkins afterwards and told him that he had gotten his facts wrong. Dan couldn't believe what he was hearing, especially since he had watched Bolt do exactly what he had described in print. "Well," Bolt sniffed. "If you were so good, you would have known that it was a 4-iron I broke, not a 5."

✔ **Go easy on the attempted psych-out.** I know plenty of guys who consider themselves to be master manipulators of the mind when it comes to playing competitive golf, and they will do lots of little things to try and psych out their opponents. Some of that is fine, to a degree. But unless you're playing on the PGA Tour or competing in the U.S. Amateur, I would suggest keeping your gamesmanship to a minimum. After all, the main idea of the sport on the club or municipal course level is to have fun, and nothing can be more aggravating than some clown who tries to take the psychological edge in your match by making you, for example, hit all the short putts that most others would concede or start talking about the divorce and child custody battle you just went through. I have met people who will evoke some obscure codicil of the rule book just as you are about to hit a shot, wondering if you may be in danger of violating some sacred edict. And others will ask you whether you inhale or exhale when you swing, just to get you thinking about anything but your swing. The ploys are numerous, they can be effective, and they can actually be funny if done in a humorous manner. But looked at seriously, that sort of behavior really is nothing more than nonsense, and I think it's practiced most frequently by pitiful, desperate souls who know not how to enjoy themselves. As a player and a person, you don't want to be like that because you don't want to ruin the game — and the day — for all involved.

✔ **Shake hands when the match is done.** Look your opponent in the eye, say, "Good match," and walk off the green together. If you have a hat on, take it off before you shake.

Good sportsmanship is a pillar of golf, and no matter how you do in a tournament, you have to play with class.

Working with the Handicap System

The United States Golf Association (USGA) created a handicap system in 1912, and the idea was to make the game more enjoyable by enabling players of all abilities to compete with each other on an equal basis. By examining the number of strokes it takes a golfer to complete an 18-hole round and making allowances for the layout and difficulty of the course, the USGA is able to determine with remarkable fairness and accuracy how many shots a player should get. What the system does, in essence, is compare a player's scoring ability to that of an expert amateur (who is expected to shoot par) on a course of standard difficulty. The higher you handicap, the more strokes you need to complete that course. The lower the handicap, the better a golfer you are.

Here's how the handicap system might work for a regular Sunday morning match at my club. Let's say I am playing with our head professional, Jack Druga, who is a scratch, or zero, handicap. That means he doesn't get any strokes. I am a 5 handicap, which means I would get 5 strokes from him during the round, one at each of the five holes that are rated highest on our course. Whatever I get on any of those holes, I subtract one for handicap purposes, and that is my net score. A gross five on the #1 handicap hole would be a four. A four on the #2 handicap hole would be a three, and so on. And on the non-handicap holes, Jack and I would be playing even.

The beauty of this system is that Jack and I can play a spirited and very even match over 18 holes because of my handicap. It gives me a chance to win against him, or at least be competitive. And it makes it possible for Jack and I to play an enjoyable game of golf with almost anyone else. No matter how good or bad they may be, as long as they have a handicap, we can make the match work.

Handicaps are determined by submitting scores into the USGA handicap system. (Many clubs and public facilities have machines that allow you to do that on-site.) You need a minimum of five 18-hole scores to get a handicap, and once you have one, you should submit every score you make to give the computer, and ultimately yourself, the most accurate reading possible on your abilities as a golfer. Don't worry if you have some bad scores; the USGA system only uses ten of your last 20 scores to calculate your handicap, and it disregards high ones that have little relation to your scoring ability.

Handicaps are important because they allow the more than 4.5 million people who have a handicap with the USGA to compete against each other better. And they are a big reason why golf is such a special game: We can all play with each other, from the best pro to the lowliest duffer.

In order for the handicap system to work properly, the handicaps have to be accurate. That means you have to turn in exactly what you got during a round. You can't turn in a higher score, which some people do in order to get a higher handicap, so they get more strokes during a match or tournament (and a better chance to win). And you can't turn in a lower score, which is what some players do in an effort to keep their handicap artificially low and impress themselves and other golfers by pretending that they're better than they really are. And you can't turn in a score if you haven't adhered to the rules of golf. In other words, if you kick your ball out of the rough a couple times during a round, if you use nonconforming equipment, if you play a round with more than 14 clubs in your bag, or if you play two balls, then you cannot use that score for handicap purposes.

Great gamesmanship at the Edmonds

When I think of gamesmanship, I cannot help but think of a day many years ago when friends Whit Foote, Jim Berrien, Henry Bertram, and I were all playing together in a member-member tournament known at our place as the Edmonds. Whit and I had teamed up in this two-day event, but we played so badly that we were out of the running before the end of the first day. Henry and Jim, however, were doing well, and as we got to the 12th green on the second day, they had a real chance of taking the title. Jim needed to make a putt of maybe four feet for par, and he squatted behind his ball to take a long look at the line, brushing away some loose bits of grass cuttings in the process. All perfectly legal, mind you. But Whit could not resist the opening. "Watch this," he whispered to me as he walked over to Jim.

"Was that living matter that you pulled out of the green, Jim, or were those old clippings?" Whit asked in all seriousness. And as expected, Jim went careening over the edge. "You know, Whit," he barked, incensed that his old friend would disrupt his concentration so. "Why do you have to do that?"

Disrupt Jim's concentration, of course, was exactly what Whit wanted to do, and he was not the least bit surprised when Jim proceeded to yank his short putt on 12 about a foot past the hole and to the left. Then he mishit his next five shots and was gone. So was the somewhat stellar team of Bertram and Berrien, thanks mostly to that little bit of gamesmanship.

I don't want to sound too dramatic here, but handicaps are a very important matter. Whether you're playing a weekend round with friends or a big tournament against top players, using a handicap that is fair and accurate is essential. Oftentimes, I've seen players show up at an event with a handicap higher than they deserve. We call those folks *sandbaggers*. They're cheaters, and as far as I am concerned, they are the scum of the earth. By doing what they do, they are cheapening a game based on honor and trust and upsetting the people they are playing with and against by breaking the rules. Fortunately, only a tiny minority of people really abuse the system in that way. And those who do are generally found out in a hurry and run out of town — or at least, off the course.

 If you have any questions about the USGA handicap system (and it can be a complicated one at times), go to the handicap section of the association's Web site at `www.usga.com/handicap/index.html`. You'll find plenty of pertinent information there. You can also ask questions of association experts as well as communicate with other golfers about the intricacies of the system.

Playing with Caddies

To me, there's nothing quite like playing golf with a caddie, and to not do that is to miss out on a very important and pleasing element of the game. Caddies are tradition and have been a part of the sport for centuries. Whether it's a grizzled, laconic Scotsman guiding you around one of the classic links courses across the pond or a young college student carrying bags during the summer to make some money for school, I've found they offer comfort and companionship to the golfer and a sense of how the game really should be played.

To say that all a caddie does is carry your golf bag, however, is to miss the point completely. A good caddie gives you yardage, cleans your clubs after each shot, and wipes off your ball once you've made it to the green (and marked it properly). He can tell you exactly how far you will hit a ball with each club in your bag (after watching you swing only a few times), and he reads a green as easily as you or I can read *See Spot Run*. He helps you find balls, and if it's a new course you are playing, he makes sure you know where to — and where not to — hit your shots.

A caddie also gives you companionship on the golf course, and it is a different sort of relationship than you have with anyone else on a layout, or probably anyone else in sports, for that matter. A caddie is your teammate and rooting section, your confidante. A good caddie makes you laugh at the right time and makes you think very clearly about your next shot. He's your mid-round therapist and knows just how to keep you from getting too high, or low, with each good or bad shot. He helps build your confidence and keep you from falling apart.

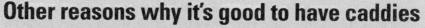

Other reasons why it's good to have caddies

At my club, we have a few older guys caddying. But the rest are local high school or college students. That makeup is not accidental; we wanted to cull most of our caddies (who, by the way, are not club employees but rather independent contractors) from those ranks. Yes, the younger caddies need more training. As a rule, they are not nearly as proficient as those veteran *loopers* (another term for caddies), and you have no hope of getting a good read on the green or accurate yardage from some of them. But by using those youths, and making sure that others do as well, we are doing something nice for our community. We're giving summer employment to a couple dozen kids. We're teaching them about the game of golf and giving them a chance to rub elbows with some very successful men and women in ways that may prove beneficial in the future, either in making important business contacts or just learning a thing or two about life. We're providing a chance at advancement for many of them, and with our new caddie scholarship program, a chance for financial aid when they head off to college. And finally, we're forging relationships with local individuals that may last a lifetime.

There are several former caddies from my club that stay in touch with members. A number of old loopers have secured good corporate jobs through the connections they made with members on the golf course. Yet they still come back to their roots. For example, I saw three or four old caddies, some of whom now work for big companies, come back to carry for our club championships last year. These guys didn't have to, but they still have great memories of their old summer job and some of the people they used to work for. And being in their 20s, they figured they could always use the extra money. It also made a lot of the members at our club feel very good a couple of years ago when two of our old caddies were invited back to play in our big member-guest golf tournament.

And he also allows you to play golf in a very reasonable amount of time. Some people swear you can play a round quicker in a golf cart. But give me a good caddie, and I can get around just as fast. And sometimes even faster.

Many of the best and fanciest clubs in the U.S. — and in the United Kingdom — have truly professional caddies. These are people who make their living at the game, and generally they are very good, though you do get some fellows who think they know it all and forget that they are supposed to work with their golfer and not show off. The people who carry your bag at Augusta National, Pine Valley, or Seminole (three of the finest private golf clubs in the world) are at the top of their field, and, as the old saying goes, they have forgotten more about golf than you or I will ever know. Many of them can really play, too.

Once upon a time, caddie programs thrived throughout the golfing world. But as the electric cart became more and more popular among a public who decided they would rather ride than walk, the use of caddies fell off dramatically. By the early 1980s, it had gotten harder and harder at most places to get any caddies, and many resorts banned walking altogether. They wouldn't even let you go out if you carried your own bag.

Fortunately, that is starting to change, and there is a growing trend among golfers toward walking in general and caddies in particular. More private clubs are starting caddie programs of their own or reviving ones that have fallen on hard times. Consider, for example, the East Lake Golf Club in Atlanta, which is most famous for being the home course of Bobby Jones. That club, which itself was in danger of closing some years ago and didn't have many caddies to speak of, has become

Caddie scholarships

The revival of caddie programs is helping bring back another of the great traditions of golf: caddie scholarship funds. I know this from experience because we recently started one at my home club. In two years, we've raised approximately a quarter million dollars that we will use to help the young men and women who serve as caddies complete their college education. You think you feel good about giving a kid $40 for a morning round and knowing that you're helping him make a living for the summer? Try being part of a group that split $30,000 in caddie scholarship money among eight caddies in one year (that's what we did in the fall of 2000) and realizing that you are making it that much more possible for them to get ahead in life. Sounds corny, I know. But it's a wonderful sensation and a very worthwhile thing to be involved with.

Many clubs, as is the case with the one I belong to, start their own caddie scholarship funds. One, called Sankaty Head on Nantucket Island in Massachusetts, actually has a caddie camp and has boarded as many as 60 youths during the summer. In addition to getting at least one loop in a day, they are given instruction in golf and trained how to caddie.

And then there are a number of organizations that have been giving out scholarships to worthy caddies for decades. The Western Golf Association's Chick Evans Foundation, named for the great amateur golfer (and former caddie) who won the 1916 U.S. Open, has provided about 7,000 men and women with college tuition and housing assistance since 1930. And the Francis Ouimet Scholarship Fund in Massachusetts, which gets its name from another one-time caddie who shocked the golf world by winning the 1913 U.S. Open at The Country Club outside Boston, has done the same for some 3,500 students since 1949. Another group worth mentioning is the Westchester Golf Association Caddie Scholarship Fund, which operates out of offices in suburban New York City and is currently helping to support 250 area caddies in schools around the country. And its four-year commitment tops $2 million.

If you have an opportunity to get involved, or contribute, to organizations like these, do it. They are great causes, and as an added bonus, they help promote golf.

a looper's dream. Currently it puts some 250 caddies a year to work on its magnificent grounds, and I can tell you from experience that they are good. Secession in Beaufort, South Carolina only opened in 1992, but it has the caddie traditions of an old-line club. The only way you take a cart there is if you have a letter from your doctor. Otherwise, you're walking. The caddie program at my club was practically nonexistent a decade ago and now we have 25 talented and hardworking loopers waiting to go every weekend morning.

A number of golf-related organizations have been helping out as well. In my part of the world, the Metropolitan Golf Association runs six, one-day caddie academies each summer, putting more than 500 kids through each one in an effort to teach them how to caddie properly and provide a trained labor force for clubs all around New York City.

Good as all that is, what's even more encouraging is that fancy resorts, many of whom had forsaken caddies in the past for much more profitable golf carts, are now seeing the light. For example, two terrific Arizona destinations, The Boulders and The Wigwam Resort, are currently offering caddies to their golfers along with their carts. And some of the finest new daily-fee layouts in the country, including spectacular Bandon Dunes in Oregon and the Whistling Straits courses in Kohler, Wisconsin, have thriving caddie programs.

It's a revolution, I tell you. A revolution. And it says a lot about a club or facility — and the people who play golf there — if they have a strong caddie program.

If you get the opportunity to play with a caddy, be sure to follow some very simple tips:

- ✔ **Always take a caddie if one is available.** Some places require golfers to take a caddie if one is around, whereas others designate times in which their use is mandated. None of that should really matter. If the club has a caddie for you, take one.

- ✔ **Ask the caddie's name early on, preferably at the first tee.** And then introduce yourself in the way you would like to be addressed during the round.

- ✔ **Let your caddie know whether you like to chat a lot or prefer to keep quiet when you play, so the caddie can act accordingly.** The good ones will pick up on that right away. The young ones won't, though I have found that many of them are usually quite deferential and will speak only when spoken to.

- ✔ **Let a caddie know whether you want him to read greens and provide yardage, or whether you will do that yourself.** At my place, which I know quite well, I will happily take yardage, but I generally prefer to read my own greens and club myself. When I am playing an unfamiliar course, however, and it has good caddies, I defer to them (unless, of course, I find their advice to be lacking, at which point I will gently let them know that I will take on those tasks myself).

✔ **Help the caddie out.** If your caddie is carrying bags for you and another player, for example, and you have hit your drives on opposite sides of the fairway, take a couple of clubs from your bag to your ball and let your caddie take care of your partner. There is no reason for your caddie to have to walk all over creation.

✔ **Treat your caddie with respect and consideration.** A caddie is not your serf or lackey. And he should not be handled that way. He is also not the person who hit that drive into the water or 3-putted on the last green. Don't abuse him, and don't blame him for your errors.

✔ **Work with younger caddies.** They are out there in most cases because they're interested in golf and want to learn. Give them a hand. Provide a little guidance and advice. If they do something wrong, don't berate them. Talk to them about their mistake the next time you're walking down the fairway together and let them know how they can correct it. They will appreciate it, and so will the next golfers who take them.

✔ **Try to avoid taking out a club when the caddie still has your bag slung on his shoulder.** Wait until he has put your bag down before you grab your weapon.

✔ **Praise your caddie if he does a good job.** Give him some credit for a good read on the green or for having the right yardage.

✔ **Buy him a drink and a snack at the halfway house or if a beverage cart comes by.** He's working hard for you, usually in warm weather, and deserves a little something for the effort. Do not, however, feel compelled to buy him a six-course meal. I say this because we had a particularly hungry fellow at our place order five different items at our halfway house one morning before the member for whom he was caddying put a stop to the madness, limiting him to just two purchases, which seemed more than reasonable. Otherwise, it sounded like he was going to have himself a Thanksgiving dinner right then and there.

✔ **Take a little time to get to know the person who is carrying your bag.** Ask some questions, be interested in who he is and what he does. That, quite simply, is good manners. He will appreciate the effort, and you will likely enrich yourself by taking the time to get to know him.

Caddies and betting

Oftentimes, the more experienced caddies like to bet a little money amongst themselves on their players in their group. And it can get a bit intense at times. I found that out the hard way some years ago when I was finishing up a round at a very nice golf club and saw my caddie wince when I missed a four-footer on the 18th hole. Naïvely, I thought he was just rooting for me. But one of the other caddies told me later on that he had $10 on that putt and was upset that I had missed it.

Not long after that incident, I heard what is still my favorite caddie story. It involves President Dwight Eisenhower and occurred when he was playing a round of golf with friends at the Augusta National Golf Club. It was getting toward the end of a very tight match when Ike putted a ball to within three feet on one of the final holes. One of his opponents, in obvious deference to the nation's commander-in-chief, said, "It's good, Mr. President." That gave him an important par, and Eisenhower, who was not a very steady putter, was delighted with the gesture. But just as he walked over to pick up his ball, his caddie said in a stage whisper, "Not by me, it ain't."

You see, the caddie was betting against his boss. And President or not, that easy par was suddenly threatening a bit of his money.

Tipping Gracefully

Tipping can be a tricky business at times because so much is contingent on where you are playing and what the general rules are at the facility. I have been to municipal layouts where no one tips anyone. And if you did, you'd get laughed off the place. And I've been to private clubs and high-end, daily-fee courses where it seems I'm handing out greenbacks all day: to the kid who opens my car door and takes my bag when I arrive, to the guys that shine my shoes and clean my spikes in the locker room, to everyone in between. In other places, there are strict prohibitions against tipping, and you never see any money changing hands between players and workers.

Your best bet is to find out what the accepted behavior regarding gratuities is at the track you're playing and follow that to the letter, especially if you're a guest at a private club. Ask your host, preferably beforehand, so you know what to expect (and whether you should put a lot of $1 bills in your money clip). If you find yourself at a club or resort still not knowing quite what to do, talk to the pro or one of his assistants. They should be able to set you straight without causing anyone any embarrassment.

When in doubt, follow these simple guidelines:

- ✔ **Tip the fellow taking care of your shoes in the locker room a couple of bucks while you are out playing.** Give him more if he does a bang-up job and sends you home with clean, polished golf shoes.

- ✔ **Tip your caddie if he does a good job.**

- ✔ **Don't worry about gratuities for anyone else.** For the most part, they are expecting — and expected — to be working on salary.

- ✔ **When you do tip people, do so as discreetly as possible.** Even if the practice is allowed, it is best not to make a spectacle of it all.

Chapter 5

This Isn't Caddyshack: Playing on Public and Private Courses

• •

In This Chapter

▶ Knowing how to handle yourself on municipal courses

▶ Setting the "country-club-for-a-day" courses apart from the rest

▶ Recognizing some additional rules for playing on private courses

• •

*I*n this chapter, I provide tips about golf etiquette as it relates to public or municipal courses; high-end daily fee tracks; and private clubs. Although golf etiquette is golf etiquette wherever you go, the particular venue you're playing does make a difference. So no matter where you're playing, read on.

Knowing the Municipal Course Basics

When I refer to municipal golf courses in this section, I'm actually talking about any facility that is open for public play (with the exception of those high-end, daily-fee tracks that are known as "country-clubs-for-a-day" and are covered later in this chapter). Some municipal courses are owned by towns and counties; others are held and operated by individuals or corporations. As a rule, the prices are low in these spots, the course conditions only fair, the variety of players extensive, the good tee times tough to come by, and the hours needed for a round on the long side. There are courses around my Connecticut hometown where it takes a 5 a.m. appearance at the start's hut to guarantee a tee time that day, and six-hour rounds are not unusual.

At municipal courses, minimum attention is generally paid to basic golf etiquette, mainly because many of the players there either don't know how best to handle themselves on a course or because they simply don't care. That's not to say all public layouts are madhouses. But it would be safe to assume that people you find on the public courses are

The many hazards of playing public courses

If you tee it up at a country club, you usually have to worry about the rules of golf a lot more than the rules of law. And no one gets that concerned about larceny or theft. But things at public courses can be different.

Consider, for example, when my friend Nat Foote, who was living in Houston at the time, hurled his 7-iron across the fairway on a local muni after a particularly bad shot. The club landed by a service road that ran through the course, and just as Nat started to walk over to pick it up, a car drove up the road and stopped by his club. Very quickly, the driver jumped out, grabbed Nat's 7-iron, threw it in the back of his car and sped away, leaving Nat in full gawk.

Now, it's not very likely that would have happened at a private club. (And, do you think Nat has ever thrown a club again?)

---

not as concerned about following all those do's and don'ts I mention in Chapter 4 as other golfers may be. The environment in that way is less structured, and there is very little peer pressure to moderate. Plus, public courses are the sort of venues where newcomers begin to work on their games, and unless they have read a book like this, they really don't know any better.

The dress code is looser at public layouts, as well, and pretty much anything goes. (One Halloween, I saw a guy teeing it up in a nun's habit on an Oregon muni.) You get all sorts of odd combinations out there that would surely make Bill Blass's worst-dressed lists — tank tops and cutoffs, sweat pants and halter tops . . . you name it, and you'll probably see it on one municipal course or another.

In general, betting is much heavier at public courses. The money got so big at the putting green at Griffith Park in Los Angeles a few years back, for example, that the police set up a sting operation and busted a dozen people or so to tone it down.

You can expect to see more beer carts at public courses as well — and more liquor consumed during the round. It's simply part of the deal.

Here are a few other tips to remember when you go out to the local course:

> ✔ **Be on time.** People jump through hoops to get tee times at many of these places, and they can lose them if everybody in the group has not shown up on time. So be there.

✔ **Treat the golf course as your own.** Sure, it really isn't yours, and it's not like a club where you have some vested financial and emotional interest in its condition. But following the unwritten rules about leaving a golf course in better shape than you found it still applies, no matter what course you're playing.

✔ **Don't assume that just because you tee it up at a muni that you should play as slowly as everyone else.** Keep pace the way you're supposed to, and maybe that steady play will help speed things up all over.

Playing at a High-End "Country-Club-for-a- Day" Course

As a rule, the courses I'm referring to here cost up to $200 or so for a round of golf, cater to a lot of business outings, have fantastic facilities, and are open to all comers. The layouts are generally of very high quality, designed by big-name architects, and kept in prime condition. Service is terrific, and so is the food and drink. In many ways they give golfers country-club facilities and treatment for a daily fee price, and they have really improved in many cases the quality of golf available to the public.

It is not unreasonable, then, to expect that the demands for etiquette and dress code at these facilities are higher than they are at most public spots, which means you should act accordingly:

✔ **Wear traditional golf clothes.** Slacks and collared golf shirts are best. No blue jeans, no cutoffs, and no tank tops.

✔ **Plan on having soft spikes on your golf shoes.** The vast majority of these courses now require that.

✔ **Stick to the unwritten rules of etiquette I list in Chapter 4.** The vast majority of the quality daily-fee tracks demand this. They want to provide "country-club-for-a-day" facilities, and they want their players to act like they are playing at such an upscale facility.

Teeing It Up at a Private Club

Of all the places you can play golf, the private club is the one that puts the greatest emphasis on the unwritten rules of etiquette and behavior — especially the really exclusive private clubs. They expect people, whether members or guests, to act in certain ways, and they're often pretty tough on those who don't toe the line.

Yes, the folks who frequent private courses can be a little ridiculous about what does and doesn't matter from an etiquette standpoint. But remember, the course is theirs, and if you want to play there, either as a member or a guest, you have to play by their rules.

However, for all the nonsense you sometimes have to put up with at big-time golf or country clubs, a pile of benefits await you. Many private clubs don't have tee times, so you can play pretty much when you want. They spend substantial amounts of money on course maintenance, so the conditioning is generally superb. Most keep the numbers of members fairly small, so the courses are rarely crowded. A number of them also have caddie programs, so you can play golf the way it was meant to be played. They are, all in all, very good places to tee it up.

So how should you handle yourself? Keep in mind that the many tips I provide in Chapter 4 and earlier in this chapter apply to private courses, too. But here are a few more:

✔ **If you're invited to a private club as a guest, be careful not to embarrass your host.** Follow your host's lead, and always ask before you do anything that may be considered even the least bit risqué. Don't, for example, pull out your cell phone at the first tee unless you know that cell phones are allowed on the course (and unless you know that your host won't mind you using one). As a rule, be subtle and unobtrusive. Clubs like people to blend into the background, and you can't go wrong if you do that yourself.

✔ **Check in with your host for a little advance guidance before you show up at his club.** Ask whether jackets and ties are required for lunch? Is it all right to wear shorts on the golf course? Is the course spikeless? Take care of these things beforehand, and you won't have to worry when you show up to play.

✔ **If you're invited to join a club and you decide to sign on, be a quiet member for a while and just observe the way the club works.** As a new member, take the time to get a sense of the club's history, if you haven't already, and the type of place it wants to be. Get to know more of the members and understand the general feel and ambience. Don't start making a lot of suggestions. Don't tell people what to do. You joined the club because you liked what it was all about, right? So why would you immediately try to change things?

My good friend Stephen Murray has the perfect five-year-plan that all new club members should adhere to, and it entails two very simple tenets: Don't show up for the first year, and keep your mouth shut for the next four. Then, and only then, should you even think about making some noise.

✔ **Never, ever, change your shoes in the club parking lot.** Few things rile a good club membership more than that. Bring your shoes into the locker room instead, and change there.

✔ **Try not to do what I did one time — drive up to the gate of the hallowed and ultra-exclusive Pine Valley Golf Club in an old truck beset with muffler problems.** Just as I downshifted into second, the vehicle backfired loudly, sending the security guard crashing to the floor of his shack, and my host, who was coming in right behind me in his car, straight to the bar. If you car isn't up to snuff, rent.

✔ **If your golf equipment isn't very good, rent that, too.** I had a friend show up at a fancy member-guest tournament one year with a pair of golf shoes that not only hadn't been cleaned or shined in weeks but also had long cuts on the sides. And his golf bag had such a gaping hole in the bottom that clubs and balls started dribbling out of it as the caddie master hauled it down to the pro shop. Some people thought the scene hysterical, especially the caddies who were infinitely amused by the balls that were bouncing down the asphalt cart path and the pro shop workers who were rushing trying to collect them. But the host member wanted to hide.

✔ **Get the lowdown on gratuities before you start handing out sawbucks like Rodney Dangerfield in Caddyshack.** Most private clubs don't allow tipping, and if they do, they expect it to be done in a discreet fashion. Pay heed.

✔ **Dress appropriately.** Golf and country clubs generally insist on collared shirts for men; women may wear collar-less ones. Men and women may wear Bermuda-length shorts as well as slacks (but no blue jeans). Tank tops, cutoffs, and T-shirts are prohibited, and so is anything that makes you look like a skate boarder instead of a golfer. You see the guys on tour on TV? That's more or less how you should look at a private club.

✔ **Know how to work with a caddie.** Help out your caddie on the course when you can. Yes, your caddie is technically supposed to be working for you. But lend a hand if the occasion calls for it. If he has to hustle a club over to your playing partner right after you have hit out of a bunker, rake the sand yourself, and give him a small break. Turn to Chapter 4 for more information on playing with caddies.

✔ **Always write a thank-you note to your host when the day is done.** Things like that mean a lot, and they are a particularly good idea if you want to get invited back.

Short shorts

One thing most private clubs don't like is golfers wearing short shorts, the feeling being, perhaps, that too much leg may bring down the empire. But there was this friend of mine who didn't cotton to that view and insisted on playing golf in a pair of short shorts that he had worn for years. He was hauled into the head golf professional's office one day for a quick (no pun intended) dressing down. It seems the pro had received a complaint about this fellow's shorts from a woman member who said they were too, ahem, revealing when he had squatted down to read a putt on the 18th green the weekend before. "You're going to have to lose the shorts," said the pro, his face helplessly breaking into a wide grin. "I don't ever want to see you out here with them on again." Then he handed my friend a brand new pair of Bermuda-length shorts as a form of inducement and added, "You can start with these."

Despite my friend's pleadings, the pro refused to tell him exactly who it was that had brought the matter of the short shorts to his attention. And as far as he was concerned, that was too bad. "I always wondered who she was," he said many years later. "I thought maybe she and I could have gone out on a date."

Chapter 6

Driving Ranges, Putting Greens, and Other Practice Facilities

In This Chapter

▶ Knowing the unwritten rules of driving ranges and putting greens

▶ Making practice into a game by betting with your friends

*J*ust because you aren't on an actual golf course doesn't mean you should throw all manners and decorum out the window. In fact, behaving properly on driving ranges, putting greens, and other practice facilities is just as important as it is anywhere else. So in this chapter I let you know how to handle yourself in those environs. (And I tell you a few funny stories in the process.)

Driving Ranges

The driving range is where golfers go to warm up before a round, correct mistakes in their swings afterwards, and work on their games in between golf outings. The driving range where I play regularly often has the social warmth of a bar or cafe, and even though I don't like to hit a lot of balls, I always enjoy going there. It's a place where people talk easily, tell jokes, toss barbs back and forth, and catch up with each other, all while they try to smooth 9-irons and crush 3-woods. To me, a certain camaraderie comes with being out on our range, especially on a weekend morning when several of my friends are down there as well. I find the whole atmosphere enchanting, even when the humor gets a little crude and the verbal assaults a little personal.

Enchanting, that is, until I watch some unthinking dolt spray one practice ball after another into the woods that run down the right side of our range. Or constantly hit outside the ropes on the tee that our golf course superintendent has laid out to designate as the hitting area for the day. There are unwritten rules (covered in the following sections) for proper range play, and making sure you're aware of them is one way you can ensure that you're a welcome sight for your fellow golfers at the range rather than the person they groan about when they see you walking up.

Watch where you're aiming

One golf pro I know used to get apoplectic when he watched members hit ball after ball into the woods abutting our driving range and never make any effort to change the way they were lined up. And that's because he was the one buying those balls every year, and when they went into those woods, they were essentially gone.

It also drove him crazy when players would hit balls in the direction of the 16th green — which was a good distance away down the left side from the practice tee, but easily reachable for bigger hitters — and the unsuspecting golfers who were lining up their putts there. "It would be blowing a gale downwind, and people would be hitting ball after ball there and bouncing them across the green," he recalls. "It didn't faze them at all. In fact, I could not believe the complete disinterest so many people had in where their balls went on the range. They didn't seem to care whether they hit anyone on 16, and it certainly didn't appear to bother them that I was losing hundreds of balls a year in the woods."

The moral here is: Be mindful of your line on the driving range. Take care where you aim. Be considerate of the pro who is buying those range balls, and of the people playing the course around the range. Oftentimes, the practice areas are shoehorned into tight spots surrounded by different golf holes, so it isn't unusual for certain shots to pose something of a hazard on occasion for golfers on the course. Take the time to know where spots are, and do your best to avoid them.

Leave the range balls on the range

I don't mean to pick on my fellow club members, but it constantly amazes me how many of them actually put range balls in their golf bags and use them on water holes (instead of the ones they bought in the pro shop). Now, I know I live in New England, and Yankees are famous for their frugality. But golf ball purchases are not going to break any of the people who play at my place. They, like everybody else, should buy the balls they use on the course, and leave the range balls where they belong — on the range.

Pay for your range balls

Many clubs and facilities leave bags or buckets of balls down at the range for golfers. The only thing they ask is that you sign a chit for those double-stripers when you use them. Now, this may not seem like a big deal for some, but I've seen plenty of players over the years upset that honor system by sneaking in a few bags or buckets for free. Don't be that way yourself. Pay for what you play.

 That brings to mind a wonderful story award-winning sports journalist Tom Callahan once told of former President Ronald Reagan and his frequent trips to the driving range at his home course at the Los Angeles Country Club in California. It seems that the Gipper used to sign a ticket for a bag of range balls whenever he would go down there. And while he was hitting shots, fellow members would walk over to the place where the signed chit was, put it in their pockets and then replace it with one bearing their own John Hancock. What they were doing was getting Reagan's autograph and then putting the balls he had intended to buy on their tab.

Hit your balls between the ropes

Most driving ranges have a pair of ropes that the golf course superintendent uses to show the areas a player may hit balls from on the tee during certain days. Do what he asks, and stay between those lines. I know, the quality of the turf outside them can look pretty tempting at times, what with the complete lack of divots usually found in the well-worn areas (and a busy driving range can get well-worn in a hurry). But the super has the area sectioned off in a certain way for a reason, and he wants to give the other areas a rest. So don't do what I see so many people at my club do, and that is purposely hit outside the ropes. It is, quite simply, bad form. And it won't help the grass out much either.

The best movie scenes involving a driving range

In Ron Shelton's film *Tin Cup,* there are several great driving range scenes, but my favorite is when Kevin Costner's character shows up at the U.S. Open and starts shanking balls down the driving range line, bouncing them off the ankles of the unsuspecting touring pros who start dancing around like their feet are on fire.

I also like one of the early scenes when Costner is describing the intricate makeup of a golf swing to Rene Russo, who is trying to figure out, among other things, how to let the big dog eat. (The big dog, of course, is another name for the driver. And one feeds the big dog by taking him out of the bag and swatting a few balls.)

Finally, there is the scene near the end of the movie in which Costner and his faithful caddie Romeo, played so ably by Cheech Marin, are tuning up for the last round of the Open early one Sunday. The morning light is low, there is dew on the grass, Costner is the only one on the range, and all you can hear is his uttering the words "dollar bills" over and over again as he hits balls, reminding himself of what it is he is playing for.

My best driving range moment

While we are on the subject, I feel compelled to share my best driving range moment with you. (After all, this is my book, isn't it?) That moment occurred a few years ago in Morocco as I was warming up for my round at the Hassan II Trophy. On one side of me was Seve Ballesteros, the Spanish pro who has won three British Opens and a pair of Masters championships. And on the other was Steve Jones, the lanky American who won the 1996 U.S. Open at Oakland Hills in Birmingham, Michigan, outside Detroit. For 20 minutes, the three of us hit one ball after another next to each other, and I was so inspired by the company that I don't believe I hit a bad shot the whole time. (But I did fall completely apart on the course later that day.)

Stay off the range when it's open

Believe it or not, I have seen some of those Yankee friends of mine actually walk off the tee and onto the range itself to collect balls when they only want to hit a few more and don't feel like paying for another bag. Balls are whizzing by their heads, yet they are so determined to save money that they don't seem to notice. They should, because they could really get hurt. A range can be a very dangerous place.

My experiences at the Hassan II Trophy, a fabulous tournament hosted by the King of Morocco each November, proved to me just how dangerous a range can be. I've had the privilege of attending the Hassan II Trophy on five different occasions; it attracts top American and European touring pros as well as dozens of well-heeled American duffers who play in the three-day pro-am. The Trophy is held at the Royal Dar Es Salaam Golf Club in the capital city of Rabat, and the vast range tee there quickly fills up with players. Problem is, the area to which the players are hitting also seems to be filled on most days with extremely courageous Moroccans who are employed by the club to gather balls off the turf by hand while players are hitting away. Usually, the workers manage to make their way through the barrage of Top-Flites without getting hurt. But I have seen a few fellows get winged over the years by hard-flying balls, and they have limped off quickly. The pain they so obviously feel for a while is the best reason of all for never going out on the range.

Putting Greens

Putting greens are located near the first tee at most golf courses. They are a place where you can hone your putting stroke and get a feel for the greens at that particular layout. (They are also the site of some unbelievably feverish betting at many municipal tracks, but more on that later.) As is the case with driving ranges, putting greens have some basic tenets of behavior that are important for all golfers to abide by, covered in the following sections.

Treat the putting green as you would any green on the course

Don't drag your feet across the putting green as you walk; doing so creates spike or scuff marks. And don't make any marks or indentations in the turf with your putter, either by leaning on it or swinging at the ground when you miss a shot.

If for some reason you do mar the surface, be sure to fix it so the next person using the green finds it in as good shape as you did.

Don't use more than a couple balls when you're practicing

Limiting the number of balls you use is simply a courtesy to other golfers who may be using the green at the same time you are. That way, you don't crowd them out by rolling Titleists all over the place. The exception, of course, is if you are the only one on the putting green. Then you should feel free to putt as many balls as you like.

Pay attention to which pin you're putting at

Putting greens usually have at least half a dozen holes with small flag-sticks at which golfers can aim. Try to avoid stroking your ball at the same pin that some other players may be aiming for. Pick one of your own.

Don't assume chipping around the putting green is allowed

Most facilities I know have a rule against chipping around a putting green, mostly because they are afraid someone will inadvertently line an errant shot into the forehead of a fellow golfer.

I can understand their concern, especially after watching a golfing friend of mine, Peter Dunn, mishit a chip shot from the edge of a practice green at a Florida club so badly that it ricocheted off the wall of the pro shop, bounced onto the roof, hopped over a garden of begonias, and landed in a woman's golf cart as she was on her way to the first tee. (He didn't even bother to retrieve his ball, or confess to the sin of hitting it as she looked around, wondering where that projectile had come from.)

Be sure to check with the pro to make sure chipping is all right before you pull out your wedge around the putting green. And if it is allowed, use the club carefully.

Use practice greens as a way to introduce the game to your kids

Practice greens are a great place to introduce the game to your children. That's where my daughter took her first swings with a golf club, and it is an easy place for kids to get initiated — and interested — in the game. It's also a fun place to hold little parent/child competitions, as the pros at my club do a couple of times each summer. They are always well-attended and always a lot of fun.

Other Practice Facilities

Essentially, practice facilities are comprised of driving ranges and putting greens, but I'm adding this brief section here because some also include what are known as *short game areas,* which have bunkers from which players can hit sand shots, and small greens up to 80 yards away to which golfers can hit different wedges. The idea here is pretty much the same as with the other areas you find at a practice facility: Take care to keep the greens, bunkers, and tees that you use in excellent shape for the next players, and watch out for your fellow golfers so nobody gets hit by one of your balls.

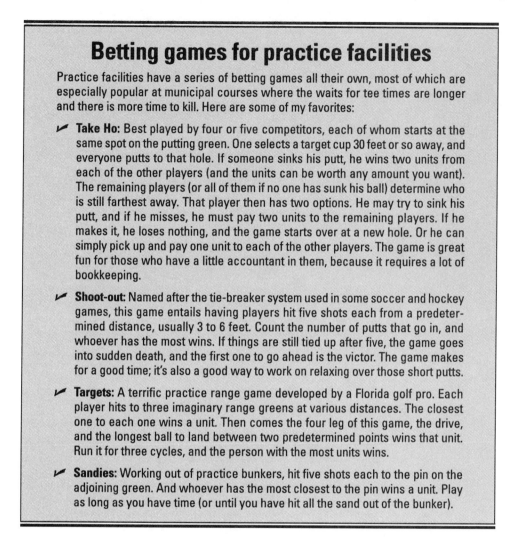

Betting games for practice facilities

Practice facilities have a series of betting games all their own, most of which are especially popular at municipal courses where the waits for tee times are longer and there is more time to kill. Here are some of my favorites:

- **Take Ho:** Best played by four or five competitors, each of whom starts at the same spot on the putting green. One selects a target cup 30 feet or so away, and everyone putts to that hole. If someone sinks his putt, he wins two units from each of the other players (and the units can be worth any amount you want). The remaining players (or all of them if no one has sunk his ball) determine who is still farthest away. That player then has two options. He may try to sink his putt, and if he misses, he must pay two units to the remaining players. If he makes it, he loses nothing, and the game starts over at a new hole. Or he can simply pick up and pay one unit to each of the other players. The game is great fun for those who have a little accountant in them, because it requires a lot of bookkeeping.

- **Shoot-out:** Named after the tie-breaker system used in some soccer and hockey games, this game entails having players hit five shots each from a predetermined distance, usually 3 to 6 feet. Count the number of putts that go in, and whoever has the most wins. If things are still tied up after five, the game goes into sudden death, and the first one to go ahead is the victor. The game makes for a good time; it's also a good way to work on relaxing over those short putts.

- **Targets:** A terrific practice range game developed by a Florida golf pro. Each player hits to three imaginary range greens at various distances. The closest one to each one wins a unit. Then comes the four leg of this game, the drive, and the longest ball to land between two predetermined points wins that unit. Run it for three cycles, and the person with the most units wins.

- **Sandies:** Working out of practice bunkers, hit five shots each to the pin on the adjoining green. And whoever has the most closest to the pin wins a unit. Play as long as you have time (or until you have hit all the sand out of the bunker).

Chapter 7

Taking Care of Business

● ●

In This Chapter

▶ Playing with clients, coworkers, and your boss

▶ Knowing how to handle winning, betting, joking, and cell phones

▶ Looking at the biggest business deals made on the golf course

● ●

Golf is not only a game of fun and recreation. To many players, it is also a critical business tool, and they often use it as a way to build relationships with their customers and coworkers and develop deals. "The sport is perfect for that sort of thing," a banker friend of mine explains as he thinks back to all the times he has taken clients out for an afternoon of golf. "First of all, by going to a golf course, you are putting yourself and whomever you are playing with in a very comfortable and attractive setting. You are together outdoors, usually in good weather and nice surroundings. Next, you are getting an audience with that person of four or five hours, which is something you would be hard pressed to achieve any other way. You also have the chance to compete together against other golfers, and that gives you the opportunity to bond together for a common cause. And you are able to really get to know someone and the way they operate, as a person and as a businessperson. To me, nothing works so well as a game of golf."

I know a lot of people who feel that way, and for that reason I give you a chapter devoted specifically to business-related golf.

Playing Golf with Your Clients

If you play business golf, your most likely companions are going to be clients, or people you would like to have as clients. Follow the simple guidelines in the following sections, and you should increase your chances of nailing that big deal.

Make sure your clients enjoy the game before inviting them

You don't ever want to put someone in the awkward position of doing something he or she doesn't really want to do. A little background check can pay a lot of dividends here and should let you know quickly whether golf is a good idea or not.

Inform your partners of the dress code and other rules

Letting your playing partners know what to expect helps put them at ease and ensures that all of you will be able to focus on the game and have a good time. Even if you know your clients have played golf before, don't assume they know the rules at the course where you're taking them. Some places, for example, don't allow men to wear shorts. Others insist that men don jackets — and sometimes ties — in the clubhouse. If that's the case, tell your client that beforehand so there is no chance of embarrassment, and so he shows up with the correct attire.

Alert your guests to things like tipping policies (most clubs don't allow tipping but the daily-fee facilities do) and whether or not soft spikes on golf shoes are mandatory (they usually are). Remember, these are your clients, and you want to take good care of them and make them as comfortable as possible.

Compliment your clients on their game

Even if he hasn't had that great a shot, offering up a compliment can't hurt. You don't want to overdo it, but there are ways to praise even the ugliest drives or chips. "That'll play," usually works. If someone is putting, you may want to holler, "One time!" if their putt looks like it has any chance of falling into the hole. It will make you sound supportive and into the game. Another innocuous but effective bit of encouragement is to ask with a certain amount of incredulity, "How did that stay out?" if a putt does just that.

Beauty is in the eye of the beholder, and if, as the beholder, you're trying to get — or keep — someone's business, your standards as to what truly constitutes a good shot are bound to go down. But hey, you have to do what you can.

Help your clients look for lost balls

Few things can be as frustrating as someone having a hard time finding a ball of his own in the rough while the other members of the foursome are off chatting by themselves. If you don't lend a hand to a client who has just put his drive in the deep rough, then what kind of a partner are you going to be if something goes wrong in a business deal?

Don't talk business every minute

I recommend that you don't even broach the subject of business until you're well into the first nine. And after that, do it sparingly.

The idea of the round is to have fun and build a relationship. Oftentimes, it is your first and best chance to get to know each other. Be patient and let things flow naturally from your game. Don't fret if you haven't cut the big deal by the end of the day. In reality, very few business sales are actually closed on the course, but an effective and efficient round can assure that they will happen shortly afterwards.

There are exceptions to every rule, of course, including this one. Be aware of what your clients really wants in this regard and follow their lead. If it seems like they want to talk business with greater intensity and regularity and possibly wrap up some sort of agreement on the course, then by all means go for it.

Don't be a teacher

Nothing is worse than having some know-it-all start handing out mid-round playing tips. It is both obnoxious and patronizing and shouldn't happen — unless, of course, your client is desperate for any kind of help and asks for your advice.

Be careful about making any comment or reference to anyone's swing. I can't begin to tell you about the times a playing companion of mine has said something like, "I am amazed you can get so much distance with such a short backswing." And guess what I am thinking about the next time I stand up to a drive? My backswing. Invariably I try to lengthen it, and invariably I hit the worst drive of the day at that very moment. If only that mindless twit had kept his thoughts on my swing to himself. . . .

That reminds me of the time I was playing a round at my home course with my good friend Nat Foote, and one of the members of our foursome felt compelled to look at Nat's putter after he had parred the third hole and say: "Is the head on that bent a little bit?" Now, Nat is a strong golfer, and he had just reeled off a quick three pars in a row. But his game died after that comment and he didn't make a reasonable putt the rest of the day. Why? Because he kept wondering if his putter head was bent or not (it wasn't) and kept making unnecessary adjustments as a result. He got so ticked off at the situation that we were sure we were going to have to medicate him, and I thought it took a tremendous amount of restraint on his part not to hurl his putter into Long Island Sound at some point during the round, or attack the well-meaning fellow who had made the comment.

The biggest business deals ever cut on a golf course

My favorite story about golf and business is one of IMG founder Mark McCormack's, and even though it happened a long time ago (in the mid-1960s), it still bears telling:

At the time, the Norfolk and Western Railroad was trying to get the U.S. rail business for the Fuji Iron & Steel Co., and as they were looking at ways to do that, they learned that the chief executive officer of Fuji was not only a rabid golfer but also a big Jack Nicklaus fan. McCormack represented Nicklaus at the time, and the Norfolk and Western people approached him about arranging a game of golf in Japan between Nicklaus and the Fuji CEO. No problem, McCormack said, and he arranged a fee of $10,000, not including expenses. Ten thousand dollars was a lot of money in those days, and not surprisingly, the IMG head was feeling pretty good about his negotiating skills. But five years later he ran into the vice president of Norfolk and Western, who said that the golf game had been very helpful. "You know," the railroad executive said. "We've done about $17 million of shipping with Fuji since then."

That showed McCormack the kind of magic golf can work in the business world. And it made him think he should have asked for a percentage of any business that came out of that round.

Going through *Forbes* magazine a couple of years ago, I read a story about Diane DeRose, an executive with Visa U.S.A., who took up golf in an effort to get ahead in her work. And one day, she landed an 18-hole round with a potential client who had declined to give so much as five minutes in the office. Once on the course, she said she managed to talk her way into a $4 billion travel account. Her conclusion: She would not have gotten the business had it not been for golf.

Reading that piece about DeRose reminds me of a story I did for *Golf Digest* magazine in the late 1990s in which I ranked CEOs of the Fortune 500 by their golf handicaps. One of the executives on that list ended up challenging the CEO who was ranked directly below him to a golf game. They had never met before, but they both had low handicaps, and they wanted to play. So they set up one match, and then another. And not too long after that, I had the chance to play a round of golf myself with one of the combatants. "I have to tell you, that article of yours was very helpful," he said as we hit balls on a driving range. "Thanks to the two games that guy and I played, we are about to sign a billion dollar partnership between the two companies." Several months later, that same executive asked the other fellow to join his board of directors. And no, I didn't receive so much as a finder's fee.

Walk whenever possible

In addition to having a general disdain for golf carts (except for those who have a medical excuse), I find them to be particularly unhealthy for business golf, and that's because they break up the foursome. If you're all walking, you can stride down the fairway together, and you can split off into different twosomes any time you want. It gives everyone a chance to be with each other. But if you have two carts, the social aspect of the game is interrupted because you have two separate vehicles tooling down the paths. Carts inhibit good interaction between players and should be avoided at all costs.

Look the other way if your client breaks a rule here or there

Golf is a game governed very strictly and appropriately by rules, and following them whenever you play is important. But when you're playing with clients, you may need to overlook a few things — especially if you're playing with a good customer.

"Unfortunately, you run into all sorts of different situations teeing it up with clients," says an investment banking friend of mine who has played in countless corporate outings. "We have guys using what we call a *foot wedge* all the time, which means they are kicking their ball out of the rough into the fairway, and even though that goes against everything you believe in, you let it go because they are your clients, and you do what you have to in order to make a sale or keep someone's business."

Playing golf with your coworkers

If you're playing a round with your coworkers, follow the same general tips for playing with clients. The hope is that your coworkers are your friends, and the occasional round of golf should be a good way to solidify those relationships. If you don't know each other, golf can be a great way to break the ice and develop that friendship.

Be careful, however, about engaging in office gossip with coworkers you don't know very well and don't say anything that may offend them (and get you in trouble with others). And because you are playing with people from your office, you need to be on your best behavior, especially with folks you are not that close to. You never know how some *faux pas* may affect you at work.

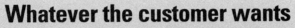

Whatever the customer wants

Consider what happened one day when a regular playing partner of mine invited two clients out to play golf at his home course. "These guys knew I liked the game and said they wanted to play sometime," he says. "So they came out, and only then did I realize how little they really knew about golf. I got them outfitted with clubs and shoes, and then I asked our golf pro to give them a quick half hour lesson so they could at least function on the course. I mean, these guys were missing shots completely and taking foot-long divots."

"So, after a while we make it to the first tee, and it is clear the lesson didn't help at all," my friend says. "They hit balls out-of-bounds or dribbled them off the tee. Finally, I got so tired of waiting, I told them just to drop in the fairway, and we were off. It took us a good half hour to get to the first green, and I wasn't sure how long I was going to have to be out there that day. But when we finished putting, they both looked at me and said, 'That's enough.' And so we went back to the clubhouse and had a drink. They loved it, and I ended up doing some business with them. But it was quite a scene."

"Actually, you cannot believe the nonsense that goes on out there sometimes, and you have to put up with it because these people are important to your business," he adds. "I have had guys blatantly cheat with the number of strokes they get in a round. I have seen people mark their ball on the green closer to the hole and ground their club in a hazard. And I never say anything to them."

In addition, my friend adds that he will go to extraordinary lengths to make sure his clients have an enjoyable round by being, for example, very generous with giving four- or five-foot putts to his client, especially if that person has had trouble making them. He also says he will let people take an extra shot if they hit a bad one and offer some sort of excuse, like saying he was talking during their back swing.

Go all out for your clients. Even if it means a day of hell on the golf course. You asked them; now you should take care of them. And who knows, it may even work out for you in the long run.

Playing Golf with Your Boss

This can be the diciest of golf rounds, the one you play with the boss. You may be a little nervous, and your game may very well reflect that. The key here is to relax and try to enjoy yourself.

What golf tells you about a person

In his best-selling book, *What They Don't Teach You at Harvard Business School,* Mark McCormack, the founder and chairman of the enormously successful International Management Group (IMG) and the father of modern sports marketing, writes about the insights he has garnered about people on the golf course over the years. A former collegiate player who started representing Arnold Palmer more than 40 years ago, he now counts Tiger Woods among his clients and has advised countless Fortune 500 chief executives on growing their companies through sports. McCormack has often said that he can tell more about how someone is likely to react in a business situation from one round of golf than he can from a hundred hours of meetings. And in his book, he takes a couple of pages to explain why.

McCormack devotes some time to psychology of the so-called "gimme" putt, a short and very makeable putt conceded to a player by his opponent. Some people, he has observed, refuse all gimmes and insist on putting everything in the hole and accurately recording their hole. McCormack's business translation: It's hard to do a favor for people like that. Other golfers don't even wait and assume a putt is given, even when it is a good distance from the cup. The business translation here is: They won't ask for a favor either, but only because they expect one. And then there are the ones who half-try to sink the putt by sweeping at it with one hand. It's fine if it goes in, and if it doesn't, well, they weren't really trying. According to McCormack, these people are hard to pin down in business, have a capacity for self-deception, tend to exaggerate, and may give you a rounded-off version of what they originally said.

Another way to peer into the mind of your business friend or foe is to ask the very simple question: "What did you shoot?" and see how he, or she, responds. McCormack tells the story of a CEO he had played golf with a number of times, and whenever he had a bad round, he always said the same thing: "I had a 79." But that 79 included a few gimme putts that rimmed the hole and a couple of memory lapses in counting up strokes. And what intrigued McCormalk most of all was that this person really believed he shot a 79. "This kind of individual makes me nervous in a business situation," the IMG founder writes. "He has the capacity for creatively interpreting facts, then sticking to them until they become gospel."

McCormack goes on to describe other incidents involving golfers and what they said about the players involved. Like those who inflate or deflate their handicap, either to have a better chance to take your money or lie about how good a player they really are. Or the ones who play fast and loose with the rules. The moral is: Pay attention. Your golfing partner may actually be telling you quite a bit about himself when the two of you play. And that could have a real impact on whether you want to end up working with him or not. In addition, it would not be a bad idea for you to be careful about how you act as well. The person you're playing with may have also read McCormack's book, or this one, and is watching just as closely.

In addition to following the rules in the preceding section on playing with clients, it is also important that you keep in mind some additional tips:

- **Don't outdo the man or woman in the corner office.** Being competitive is okay, but not to the point at which you're embarrassing the person who signs your paychecks. Be subtle with your celebrations. Be fair with your rulings. Be humble with your successes. And be reasonable with your behavior.

  Keep in mind that you don't have to roll over for your boss. In fact, if you don't try your best and play your hardest, your boss will likely be offended. He or she will actually respect you more for doing your best than if you throw the game.

- **Play precisely by the rules.** You should do this anyway, of course. But if you cheat in front of your boss on the golf course, then imagine what he or she may think about the numbers on those hefty expense accounts you keep turning in.

- **Watch what you say.** Measure every word and utterance. Yes, you are out on the golf course to have fun. But you are also playing with your boss, so you need to be careful with what you blurt out.

Understanding the Do's and Don'ts of Some Key Issues in the Game of Golf

The following bits of advice apply to all games of golf you may play. But they are of particular importance to those rounds that have a business bent.

Winning

Being a good winner is important. Do it gracefully. Never rub defeat in someone's face, and never gloat over a great shot or hole. Smile, chuckle, enjoy the moment when you drain a big putt or leave an 8-iron within inches of the pin. But don't overdo it.

Betting

I cannot think of a round of golf I've played in the last 20 years when there wasn't some amount of money riding on the outcome. Betting is an inherent part of the game, and there is nothing wrong with a little Nassau among friends or business associates. But keep it friendly and loose. And keep the stakes low. No one will be impressed with how much money you want to bet on a golf course, or how often you want to bet it.

ANECDOTE

Big talk and high stakes

When I think of golf course betting, I always remember a story told about Jack Stephens, the Arkansas investment banker who served for a time as chairman of the Augusta National Golf Club. Legend has it that Stephens was playing at that hallowed venue one day in a foursome that included a boorish business tycoon who spent much of his round talking about how much money he was worth (say, $40 million) and how much they bet at his course back home. "Hell, we play $1,000 Nassaus all the time, and the junk gets pretty pricey, too," he said. "I don't know why you all stick to this nickel-and-dime stuff down here."

Now, Jack Stephens is a soft-spoken man who was worth some $600 million at the time, and he put up with that fellow's incessant chatter for as long as he could. But back in the clubhouse, as the bets were paid off, the guest began making noise again about the big money he played for at his home course. And he did this as he shuffled a deck of cards. So Stephens looked over at him slyly and asked, "How much did you say you were worth?" And after the man gave the amount, the Augusta chairman said, "I'll cut you for it."

Not surprisingly, the room got awfully quiet after that.

Telling jokes

Go easy when it comes to telling jokes, especially if you're a guest of your boss or someone important to your work. There is no better place for classic story telling and bawdy jokes than a golf course. And there have been many times when my playing partners and I have gotten so tickled over some hysterical story that we literally had to wipe tears from our eyes before we could take a swing at the ball.

But when you're playing for business, be sure to stay away from any jokes that could offend people in your group. A bad joke can easily offend and ruin an otherwise good round, to say nothing of what it could do to the business relationship.

Drinking

Drinking is another area of concern, and with good reason. Too many drinks before, during, or after a round can cause significant problems at the workplace. And it won't do your driving home any good either.

My advice here is follow the lead of your host. Wait to see what he does, and then go from there. That doesn't mean you have to toss down one shot after another just because the potential client you really want is doing it. But if your client has a beer after a round, don't be afraid to have one yourself if you would like. If, however, your client orders lemonade, hold off on the booze. For one thing, he could be a teetotaler, and any alcoholic consumption may offend him. Or maybe he has a drinking problem, and your drinking may make him feel uncomfortable.

Plus, if you're the only one drinking, you may end up yapping too much after a drink or two (that's why my friends and I have long called alcohol *loudmouth soup*) and saying something you could regret later.

The best players to get for corporate outings

Some companies hire touring pros to come to their golf outings to give lessons, tell stories, and play in some of the groups. Oftentimes, these can be huge fun for the participants, and very effective ways of securing business for the corporate host.

I have played in several outings like that over the years, and I recommend going to one if you're lucky enough to be invited. And I hope that, for your sake, you get paired with one of the following players, who are great partners on the golf course and willing to spend time with and work hard for their hosts and guests.

- ✔ **Arnold Palmer:** Still the King in most people's eyes, Palmer is a lovely fellow to be around. He always has time for his fans and is regarded as one of the best partners an amateur hack could ask for.

- ✔ **Pete Jacobsen:** A longtime PGA Tour player, Jacobsen has charm, warmth, and terrific people skills. He makes everyone feel comfortable and never fails to amuse.

- ✔ **Billy Casper:** A two-time U.S. Open winner, Casper still feels lucky to have had such a great career in golf and acts that way. He's a hugely popular draw who can tell a good story.

- ✔ **Gary Player:** Player loves to talk and loves to make friends. He has an amazing ability to make everyone feel special. And he will give you fitness tips as well.

- ✔ **Gary McCord:** The author of *Golf For Dummies,* McCord is a real cutup n the course, and he does dozens of corporate outings a year, so he knows how to make it fun for all involved. The best part is, he really seems to enjoy it.

- ✔ **Nancy Lopez:** Perhaps the best player in LPGA history, Lopez is very popular on the outing circuit and in great demand. She has a great game and a great personality to match.

- ✔ **Nick Price:** Price is one of the good guys in professional sports, and the sort who will sit down and have a beer with you after a round. He's an awesome ball striker, and it's hard to believe that someone in his position could be so nice.

- ✔ **Nancy Scranton:** One of the top players on the LPGA tour and terrific fun on the golf course, Scranton is very comfortable with amateurs and goes out of her way to make them feel the same way.

Golf school for executives

With golf becoming such a big part of the business world, major American corporations have taken to sending their executives to golf schools so they can become proficient not only in the game but also in cutting deals and closing sales on the course. IBM, General Motors, and Gillette are among the growing number of Fortune 500 companies who have taken to doing this, spending thousands of dollars in some cases so their workers know what they are doing out on the links. Clinics not only cover basic swing techniques but also show the golf neophytes how to dress and act on a course while teaching them a bit about golf's history and culture.

Wouldn't it be less expensive — and more effective — if they all just bought copies of this book?

If you're the host, offer your guests a drink as a matter of courtesy. But don't push the booze on anyone, and don't make them feel uncomfortable if they do, or do not, have a pop.

Cell phones

Don't bring cell phones out to the golf course. They don't belong there, and neither do you if you can't get through a round without putting one to your ear. Nothing is more obnoxious than some phone ringing in a player's bag in the middle of your back swing or having to listen to a self-important lout bark sell orders to his assistant while the rest of your group is lining up their putts. It is especially bad during a business round, with your boss, perhaps, or maybe some clients. It does not say a lot about your feelings to them if you keep interrupting conversations and that critical relationship-building to answer calls. That will serve only to alienate, and also distract, your playing partners.

Are there ever exceptions? Well, in this case I can think of two: if you are a doctor on call and may have to respond to an emergency, or if your wife is pregnant and about to have your child. Otherwise, leave the phones at home.

Part III

Even More Rules . . . For Players and Spectators

The 5th Wave   By Rich Tennant

"The book said before teeing off, I should make sure the ball is opposite my left armpit. So I put it in my right armpit, but it's heck trying to get a piece of the ball from there."

In this part . . .

The next best thing to playing golf is watching other people play, particularly the pros. But being a spectator at a tournament isn't as simple as just showing up. You have to know how to conduct yourself in a manner befitting this great game. And in the chapters in this part, I show you exactly that.

Chapter 8

The Do's and Don'ts
of Golf Outings

* *

In This Chapter

▶ Behaving at business outings

▶ Knowing the ins and outs of charities events

▶ Playing in pro-am tournaments

* *

*N*ot all the golf you play is going to be weekend rounds with your usual group. Especially now that the game has become such a popular business, entertainment, and fundraising tool. Business and celebrity outings, as well as charity events and tournaments are as big a part of golf these days as the country club member-guest or the Sunday morning four-ball match at the local layout. And knowing what to do — and what not to do — is important.

Business-Related Golf Outings

Golf outings have become a staple of doing business in the U.S. and a way for executives, customers, and their associates to build relationships, cut deals, and have fun in the process. The popularity and proliferation of these sorts of events prove that they often work wonders. But they do not necessarily attract the most stringent followers of golf rules and etiquette or always induce participants to adhere to those codes. In fact, business-related golf outings often have a bit of the Wild West in them.

Consider, for example, the following comments from a top amateur golfer I know who has not only played in dozens of those events over the years but also runs one of his own. "There are no real rules or etiquette in most business outings," he says. "Guys show up in sneakers, pull out cell phones every other hole, kick balls out of the rough, and spend half their time trying to flag down the beer cart. It can be a very different game, and anything goes."

Business outings often go that way because not all the invitees know a lot about the game of golf. And the host may have a hard time doing anything when someone behaves badly — whether intentionally or not — because the he is trying to schmooze the very people he has asked to the outing. Even Emily Post would admit that chastising someone for various breaches of rules or etiquette on the golf course is not the best way to further your entertainment goals. "So you have to put up with a lot," says a friend of mine who has organized a number of business outings of his own. "I am not going to jump all over an important client when he pulls out a cell phone at a club that does not allow their use or doesn't replace a divot, because none of that is going to help me get his business."

Unfortunately, those realities can make business outings a somewhat difficult endeavor for those golfers who fervently believe in the rules and etiquette of the game. And it can make it tough for someone who, frankly, doesn't know any better. But none of that means you or anyone else should throw all respect for golf rules and etiquette out the window just because others have. Knowing how to act at a business outing is important, even if others don't.

So how should you act? Well, my friend Jack Druga, a PGA golf professional at the Country Club of Fairfield in Fairfield, Connecticut, offers a sensible list of do's and don'ts that bears some studying:

- ✔ **Respect the course you are playing.** Replace divots, fix ball marks, and rake bunkers. Make sure you leave it in as good shape as you found it in.

- ✔ **Remember that you are a guest of the club where the outing is being held, and you need to behave that way.** Take the time before you go to find out the club's specific rules, and then follow them. Be aware of the dress code. Some clubs don't allow men to wear shorts, most prohibit men from going out with collarless shirts, and only the most relaxed clubs allow blue jeans or sneakers. If the club policy is no cell phones, then don't use yours. Don't pass out handfuls of greenbacks as tips to the staff if there is no tipping (and many clubs do not allow tipping).

- ✔ **Buy something from the pro shop.** Even if it's just a sleeve of balls. Buying from the pro shop is a way of thanking the club's golf pro. The pro will appreciate the gesture, because purchases like that are one way he makes his living.

- ✔ **Make sure you thank the staff who ran the event and helped out.** Outings require an enormous amount of work, and the men and women who put them together often run themselves ragged trying to accommodate everyone. A little bit of gratitude goes a long way.

- ✔ **Be understated.** Golf is not a game for the immodest and ostentatious. Keep it toned down in dress and demeanor, and you'll do just fine.

Knowing how to respond to celebrities

Many of the same rules apply in celebrity golf outings as apply in outings conducted for business purposes, but there is also the issue of dealing with the celebrities who are competing in the same event. Taking photos and asking for autographs are fine to an extent, but be sure you don't smother the celebs with requests and unwanted backslapping. Don't be afraid to approach them, talk to them, or joke with them. After all, that's the main reason they are at the outing, and some interaction is expected on both parts. Just be careful not to overwhelm anyone. Have fun, treat the stars with respect, and nine times out of ten, they will do the same for you.

Jack's list is one worth saving. And it wouldn't hurt if we added a few more items:

- ✔ **Use the correct handicap.** No one likes a cheater, and there is no reason to fudge on the number of strokes you should be getting.

- ✔ **Play by the rules.** Some people figure that it doesn't matter whether they give themselves that 5-foot putt or improve their lie in the fairway because "it's only an outing." But it is still golf, and it should be played that way.

- ✔ **Be careful how much you drink, especially if your boss is around.**

- ✔ **Show up on time.** I had a good friend lock his keys inside his car while he was visiting his latest love interest the night before a big outing, and he didn't realize his mistake until the following morning. It took his emergency road service an hour to arrive, and my friend didn't make it to the course until the group he was supposed to be playing in was on the 9th tee. Needless to say, his partner was not at all amused after having had to play the first eight holes by himself. And he didn't find it the least bit funny when my friend, badly hung over and still stinking of gin, snap-hooked his first drive into the weeds and asked if he could have a mulligan. (The caddies, however, fell over in laughter.)

Charity Golf Outings

Anyone playing in a charity golf outing would do well to study the list that Jack Druga put together (see the preceding section). But there are a few other things to keep in mind:

- ✔ **Feel free to exchange any gifts you're given.** Every charity outing has a goody bag of gifts, which usually comes from the pro shop at the host club. Don't be afraid to exchange anything you have gotten after the event. The pro doesn't care, because you are still getting something from him. And the organizer, quite frankly, is just glad you came (and paid your requisite fees).

✔ **Participate in games and raffles.** Charity events usually have a collection of raffles and games that the organizers use in hopes of raising even more money. Support them generously as well. After all, it's for a good cause.

✔ **When it's time to go to the tee, go to the tee.** Too many times players operate on their own schedule and not the tournament's. They head to the practice range or linger on the putting green when they should be off with their group. Be ready to start playing when the horn blows.

✔ **Keep a good pace of play.** Outings of this sort invariably take longer to play than your basic weekend match, and that's because too many of the participants insist on playing their seventh and eighth shots when they should have picked up long ago. Don't make matters worse by doing that yourself. When you are out of a hole, put the ball in your pocket and root for the other members of your team.

✔ **Be aware of the cause your are supporting.** Don't light up a cigar, for example, if the event you are playing in benefits cancer research. And don't expect to find a beer cart at a tourney that in raising money for a local rehab center.

Pro-Am Tournaments

Pro-ams (short for professional-amateur tournaments) are events in which touring pros play with amateur golfers as teams in what are often pre-tournament competitions (though some do include rounds that actually count for the pros). They last anywhere from one to four days, and can cost as little as $500 a person or more than $10,000 to enter. They also provide one of the great thrills in sports, because what other game allows amateurs to play with professionals? Ever hear of any of your friends shooting hoops with Michael Jordan or running pass patterns for Kurt Warner? No, because that sort of thing doesn't happen in basketball, football, hockey, or baseball. But it does in golf, thanks largely to a handicap system that makes it possible for rank amateurs to play with Tiger Woods, Karrie Webb, and other tour stars.

Most pro-ams take place on Wednesday, the day before the professional tournament begins and a time when the folks on tour are mostly concerned with getting in a little practice. But some events, like the AT&T Pebble Beach National Pro-Am and the Bob Hope Chrysler Classic last longer. And consequently, the intensity — and the stakes — can get a bit high because every stroke a pro makes not only counts for his team of amateurs but also — and more importantly — for the event in which he is competing.

So if you are going to play in a pro-am (and they really are huge fun), remember these important points:

✔ **Make sure you are a good enough golfer and know enough about the game to play a decent round and not cause anyone any problems or embarrassment on the course.** No one is asking for you to play at scratch. But players should have a handicap, some tournament experience, and a good understanding of the rules and etiquette of the game before entering a pro-am. Otherwise, the experience simply won't be a pleasant one for all involved.

✔ **Pick up your ball if you are out of the hole.** Nothing aggravates a pro more than an amateur who insists on putting out for his seven when the team has a net-three all set. The rule is, if you can't make better than a net par, then put the ball in your pocket and move on.

✔ **Make sure that you, your caddies, and your partners don't move or talk when your pro is playing, and keep out of his way as he hits his shots.** Show the pro the utmost respect out on the course. Remember that this is where the pros make their living, and even if it is a practice round, they're still trying to concentrate on things that can make the difference in winning or losing thousands of dollars of prize money.

✔ **Don't badger your pro with dozens of photograph and autograph requests.** You can ask for some (it's expected), but too much can get very, very tiresome. Pros sometimes talk abut being *ammed out* (sick of playing with amateurs). Try not to be the one who does that to your guy. (And if you see one of your playing partners starting to get that way, tell him to back off as well.)

✔ **Relax and have fun.** Playing with someone who drives the ball 60 yards past you or never misses a green with her irons (while you miss every one) can be a bit intimoidating. Don't worry; that's why they're pros. Just play your game and do what you can to help the team.

Pros are people like everyone else, and some are better at this pro-am game than others. Unfortunately, there are players on the tour who just can't let loose enough to have fun with their amateurs. It's "Hello" on the first tee, "Good-bye" on 18, a few "Nice shots" in between, and that's it. But the vast majority of the pros are extremely good at making their amateurs feel welcome. They'll tell jokes, dole out playing tips, give you high-fives, and help you read putts. The key is this: Treat your pro with consideration and respect, and the pro will likely do the same for you.

The five best pro-ams

Almost every professional golf tournament has them, but our friends in the game say these are the ones you really want to play:

✔ **AT&T Pebble Beach National Pro-Am:** The creme de la creme of this kind of golf outing, the AT&T Pebble Beach National Pro-Am first gained its fame as Bing Crosby's Clambake, and the crooner's Hollywood buddies would all show up. Started in San Diego in 1937, the event moved to the Monterey Peninsula in 1953 and has been there ever since. Crosby's name hasn't been attached to it since 1985, but the tournament is still a must-play. Why? Its history, for one thing. Also, amateurs get at least three days of golf and play on some fabulous courses, including Pebble Beach. No event has such a flashy group of celebrities ("You're away, Mr. Costner"), and the parties are pretty good, too.

✔ **Bob Hope Chrysler Classic:** This is another great tournament with four days of golf on some of the best courses in the Palm Springs area. The Hope has history, beautiful weather in the winter, lots of parties, and a good complement of celebrities from both the sports and entertainment worlds. In addition, it always attracts a very strong field of touring pros at a time when they are fresh and the new season is just starting up.

✔ **Nabisco Championship:** One of the things that makes this two-day, LPGA pro-am so good is that it is one of that tour's Grand Slam events. The best women players in the world show up to compete at Mission Hills in Palm Springs, and that means good pairings for the amateurs. It also means plenty of topflight stargazing because celebrities flock to this event, not only to play but also to entertain. In 1999, for example, Celine Dion sang at the big pro-am dinner, and years ago, when the tournament bore Dinah Shore's name, she used to coax people like Frank Sinatra into stopping by for a song. The prizes are deluxe, the social events happening, and the desert setting first-rate. Plus, there is the added bonus of playing with players from the women's tour, who many amateurs say are better than their male counterparts at relating to weekend golfers and making sure they have a great time.

✔ **Electrolux USA Championship hosted by Vince Gill and Amy Grant:** Held at the Legends Club of Tennessee in Nashville, this LPGA pro-am is a favorite thanks mostly to the star quality that Gill and Grant bring to it as Country & Western's first couple and the great entertainment they and their friends provide. The event lasts for two days, and when the golf is done (at one of the state's finest tracks), there is much music to listen to (and a bit of bourbon and branch water to drink). Plenty of Nashville's music community plays in the pro-am, and Gill and Grant, both of whom are fanatical golfers, go all out.

✔ **Hassan II Trophy:** This is easily the most exotic of the pro-ams — and certainly one of the most exclusive in the world. Started by the late King Hassan II of Morocco in 1971 and staged on the superlative Red Course at the Royal Dar Es Salaam Golf Club in the capital city of Rabat, it attracts pros from both the American and European men's and women's tours and includes a couple of black-tie dinners and ten days of fun in the North African kingdom. Participants get to eat, drink, play, and travel with the pros; rub elbows with Moroccan royalty; and experience everything from the souks in Marrakech to the ancient Roman ruins at Volubilis. Locals feel that anyone who plays in the Hassan II Trophy is a guest of the King (now the late monarch's eldest son, Mohammed VI), and competitors are treated royally at every turn.

Chapter 9

Keeping Your Cool on the Course: Fan Etiquette

● ●

In This Chapter

▶ Knowing how to act at golf tournaments

▶ Being familiar with how the Masters works

▶ Asking for autographs politely

● ●

Golf etiquette is not limited to the people who actually play the game. There are also lots of do's and don'ts for the folks who go out to watch tournaments in person, whether it's a Grand Slam event for one of the three major professional tours in the U.S. or a local amateur contest. And these events demand a more moderate kind of behavior than is generally found, say, in the stands of a Major League baseball game, where blowing air horns and heckling athletes are an accepted part of the fun.

Attending Golf Tournaments

Nothing in sports is quite as enjoyable as attending a professional golf tournament, or even a tournament that pits top amateur players against each other. It gives you the chance to observe the best players in the world up close and personal and see exactly how they are able to crush 300-yard drives and drain 30-foot putts. You can get so near the action (see Figure 9-1) that you can actually hear them talk to their caddies, talk to each other, and even talk to their balls as they try to coax a bit more fade or draw from their shots. You can follow your favorite golfers around the course, and you can also watch them hit balls on the practice range or work on their strokes on the putting green. No other athletic pursuit gives you things like that from such an accessible and enjoyable fashion. So if you have the chance to attend a tournament, I have only one word for you: Go!

Figure 9-1: Attending golf tournaments gives you the chance to get up close to the best players in the world, like these fans are doing with Tiger Woods.

But if you do go, you have to be aware that fans are expected to act in certain ways at golf tournaments so as not to disturb the competitors or the spectators around them. Unlike many sports, golf has a code of etiquette for spectators that you need to understand. And although the exact guidelines may vary from event to event, you will never go wrong if you adhere to these simple edicts:

- ✔ **Be quiet when players are addressing their balls and swinging their clubs.** And watch the noise even when they have completed their shots. Sounds carry easily on a golf course, especially if it's windy and there are not a lot of trees. What you say on one fairway may be heard quite clearly on another one 100 yards away. The group you're watching may have finished, but someone on the next hole may be getting ready to hit.

- ✔ **Don't move when a player is addressing or hitting a ball (see Figure 9-2).** And always make sure to look around carefully before you do move so that you know you will not disturb someone in the process. Movement can be terribly distracting to players, and they really appreciate fans who are extra careful about that.

- ✔ **Wait for all the players to finish hitting before you move.** This is a very big problem these days with all the people following certain players, like Tiger Woods, around the course. Spectators are sometimes inclined to leave the green or tee after Tiger has hit his shot instead of waiting for the other members of Tiger's group to play. Give every golfer the same respect, and make sure he doesn't have to hit his next shot while you and dozens of other spectators are fleeing to another spot.

Figure 9-2: Remain quiet and still when a player is hitting his ball, like these courteous fans.

- ✔ **Don't run around a golf course.** That's a big no-no at Augusta National and other venues. There is no rush on the links, and no fire. So move at an orderly pace, even if the skies open up and a downpour ensues.

- ✔ **Do not, under any circumstances, holler, "You Da Man!" after someone has hit his drive.**

- ✔ **Leave your cell phone and camera at home.** Cell phones are a general nuisance, and they are prohibited at most golf events, with good reason, I might add. They beep in the middle of back swings and just as putts are about to be hit. And there is nothing more obnoxious than listening to some self-important jerk bark at an underling on the phone while you and others are trying to figure out how Nick Price is going to hit a certain shot. My view on cell phones is quite simple: If you cannot stand to be without yours for a few hours or are simply too busy to be gone from work for so long, then don't bother showing up at the golf course. Clearly, if you can't afford or handle the time away from your precious phone, you would be doing the players and your fellow fans a favor by staying home.

The same is true of cameras, which are also banned from most tournaments but are regularly pulled out just the same. Cameras can cause real problems on their own. Consider, if you will, the 2000 Tour Championship at the East Lake Golf Club in Atlanta, Georgia. It was Saturday afternoon, the third round, and Tiger Woods and David Duval were playing in the same group. Duval lined up a 10-foot par putt on the 10th hole and was getting ready to hit it when some moron from the crowd took a flashbulb photograph. Duval backed off the ball, took another look at the putt, and then tried again. Unfortunately, it ended up doing a 360-degree spin around the hole and stayed out for a bogey. Later, Duval spoke for many professional golfers when he said, "It's a shame people don't give you the courtesy you deserve when you're trying to compete."

In general, contrary to the man shown in Figure 9-3, the behavior of golf fans is far and away better than that of spectators of most other sports.

Figure 9-3: Golf spectators are among the best-behaved of the sports-watching crowd. Maybe this fan meant to go to a football game instead.

But the game has recently been undergoing some dramatic changes in that regard, in large part due to a great influx of new fans. Their emergence is part of what is called the *Tiger factor,* and it has mostly benefited golf. Attendance of PGA Tour events, for example, has never been

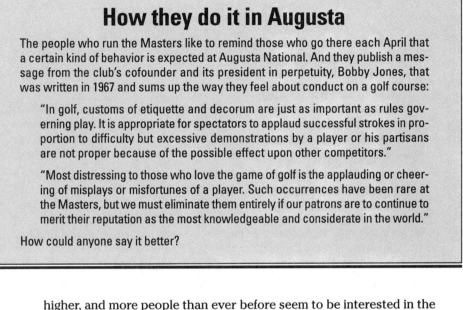

How they do it in Augusta

The people who run the Masters like to remind those who go there each April that a certain kind of behavior is expected at Augusta National. And they publish a message from the club's cofounder and its president in perpetuity, Bobby Jones, that was written in 1967 and sums up the way they feel about conduct on a golf course:

"In golf, customs of etiquette and decorum are just as important as rules governing play. It is appropriate for spectators to applaud successful strokes in proportion to difficulty but excessive demonstrations by a player or his partisans are not proper because of the possible effect upon other competitors."

"Most distressing to those who love the game of golf is the applauding or cheering of misplays or misfortunes of a player. Such occurrences have been rare at the Masters, but we must eliminate them entirely if our patrons are to continue to merit their reputation as the most knowledgeable and considerate in the world."

How could anyone say it better?

higher, and more people than ever before seem to be interested in the game. The problem is that many of the newcomers don't know or understand the nuances of the game, even as it relates to being a spectator. And that lack of knowledge has led to many more incidents like that one David Duval had to endure at East Lake. Obviously, the person with that camera didn't mean any harm by what he did. But the fact is that it did harm Duval, and it is something that would not have happened had that shutterbug been following the do's and don'ts of fan etiquette. Says one PGA Tour insider: "Sadly, we have been seeing more and more of that sort of thing in golf. In fact, I think that fan behavior has gotten a lot worse because we now have so many non-knowledgeable golfers attending events. They simply don't know that much about the game, and they don't really know how to act. We will continue to have our share of problems until our fans understand what they can and can't do."

So make it a point to know those things before you head out to the links.

Desperately Seeking Autographs

Autograph hunting (see Figure 9-4) has long been a part of the tournament golf scene, and a goodly number of spectators like to clamor for the signature of their favorite player. That's fine, with plenty of caveats.

The best behaved crowd

You will find the best behaved crowds at Augusta National. For one thing, many of those attending the Masters have been going to golf tournaments for years, so they know the game and they know the ways they are supposed to act around it. It is a very traditional golf crowd.

Secondly, there is a great deal of peer pressure to behave well from other fans at Augusta, because minding your manners is extremely important to so many who attend the event. If you break into a run between holes or pull out a cell phone, you will get very severe stares and sometimes even an admonishment from other fans.

Finally, the people who run the tournament make it very clear that they take golf course behavior seriously. Spectators lose their badges (tickets) if they act badly, and the powers at Augusta are not the least bit shy about enforcing the rules. That, perhaps, is the greatest deterrent, because people know that if they step the least bit out of line, they will lose what is considered one of the toughest tickets in sports. But it is also one of the things that makes the Masters a lot of fun to attend. The crowds there are always good.

The galleries at Jack Nicklaus's Memorial Tournament at his Muirfield Village Golf Club in Dublin, Ohio, are excellent as well. They, too, seem to have a special appreciation for how the sport should be viewed from outside the ropes and comport themselves beautifully.

© L.C. Lambrecht

The worst behaved crowd

The mob at the Phoenix Open is, hands down, the worst anywhere. Held each winter at the Tournament Players Clubs (TPC) of Scottsdale, it regularly attracts record number of fans (more than 400,000 over the four-day event) who ply themselves with buckets of beer and give the event a sort of a rock concert atmosphere. Things get particularly bad at the par-3 16th hole, where the largest crowds are concentrated. "That hole has become a sort of crucible for players," says Brian Hewitt, my colleague at *Golfweek* and a terrific chronicler of life on the PGA Tour. "They walk off the 15th green and through a throng of people to the 16th tee, and it is like going into the Colosseum. The people in the crowd are like lions and fans at the same time. Sometimes they smell blood, and unless a player is very popular and very smart and knows how to play to that crowd, it can get pretty rough."

How rough? A few years ago, as a newly-sober John Daly was getting ready to hit his drive on 16, someone yelled, "Hey, John, want some vodka?" Then there was the incident with Casey Martin, the young golfer with the circulation problems in his leg that cause him to walk with a severe limp and necessitate his riding a golf cart in order to compete. His drive on 16 came up short one time, and a fan hollered, "Hey, Casey, walk it off." It got so bad there during a recent event that David Duval considered withdrawing, saying, "I simply believe that we as players should be treated with a little more respect." Other comments about Phoenix include one golf writer bemoaning the lack of arrests for bad behavior at the tournament by saying, "Getting thrown out of the Phoenix Open is harder than getting thrown out of reform school." And then, of course, there is Hal Sutton's line. "I think there is a pretty damn good party going on here," he said one year. "But there's a golf tournament lost somewhere in the middle of it."

Phoenix reached a real low in 1999 when police arrested a rowdy fan in Tiger Woods's gallery and found that he had a gun in his fanny pack. The man did have a permit, and there was no evidence that he had any intention of using the weapon. But it was an alarming incident nonetheless.

Be considerate when you ask a golfer for his or her autograph. "Players are usually more than happy to oblige," says a longtime tournament director from one of the professional tours. "But they do get upset when people do not ask nicely. In fact, you would have a hard time believing how many fans don't ask for an autograph, they demand one. People can be so rude at times, and it doesn't take much to earn the appreciation of a player. They like it when fans ask nicely, and they like it when people say thank-you. They also like the fact that whatever it is they're signing is going to be used for personal reasons and not for resale."

© L.C. Lambrecht

Figure 9-4: Be considerate when you're seeking autographs from the players, and you'll be rewarded in turn. Tiger Woods and Jack Nicklaus are two fan favorites.

The next questions that come up most often with autographs are when and where you can ask for them. At many tournaments, such as the Masters, spectators are not allowed to ask for autographs on the course, and players are not allowed to give them there. Instead, special places are set up for just such an exchange, usually off by the locker room or practice area. (At the Masters, it's on the parking lot side of the clubhouse, near the range.) Find out the policy of the place you are visiting and adhere to it.

As for *when,* my friend the tournament director thinks the practice days (Tuesday and Wednesday) are best because players are most relaxed then (though it is not always good to home in on the player during the pro-am, when he is supposed to be entertaining his amateurs). During the actual event, wait until the players have putted out on 18 and are walking off the course, assuming, of course, that this fits in with tournament guidelines. Remember that the golf course is where the players do their work, and to compete on any of the professional tours is an enormous accomplishment that requires the utmost concentration. One or two strokes can make the difference between a big payday and nothing. So wait until the players have punched their clock before hitting them up for their autographs.

Be aware, my friend adds, of what the pros you are approaching have shot. "It is not a good idea to go up to some guys right after they have posted a 78," he says. "They usually don't want to be bothered by anyone at that point, and you can understand that. As for the guy who just shot 66, he'll usually sign for an hour."

There is also one more thing for autograph seekers to consider: Be careful about jabbing your pens and markers at the pros you want to have sign your balls or programs. Too many times the players feel that they are about to be skewered like a piece of meat for a shish kebob when they see those things being shoved at them. Many have taken to wearing dark shirts when they know they are going to be besieged so the ink that invariably ends up on their shirts is not quite so noticeable.

Part IV
The Part of Tens

The 5th Wave   By Rich Tennant

©RICHTENNANT

Hey! You're supposed to rake the sand after you're in the bunker! I'll bet I know who did this, too. I'll bet it was that new club member. You know, the big guy.

In this part . . .

This wouldn't be a ...*For Dummies* book without The Part of Tens. Here you find information on the worst penalties in the game (the ones you want to avoid at all costs), as well as tips for playing some of the best betting games in golf. Finally, I end the part by paying homage to the great golf films of our day, including *Caddyshack* and *Tin Cup.* So if you're in a hurry but you still want to read up on the game or have a good laugh, you've come to the right part.

Chapter 10

The Ten Most Devastating Penalties

In This Chapter

▶ Being aware of penalties

▶ Avoiding penalties at all costs

*G*olf is such a precise game and the margin of error so great that any penalty can have monumental impact on a round or tournament. Obviously, getting disqualified is the worst punishment, and there are plenty of ways that can happen to suspecting — or unsuspecting — golfers. Sign an incorrect scorecard for a number lower than the one you actually shot, and you're gone. No more tournament. No more chances for a big win. And, as the Dean of Faber College said in *Animal House* when he was threatening some of his rowdier charges, "No more fun of any kind!"

But even a 1- or 2-stroke penalty, which is what you get for lesser violations, can be significant, because tournaments are often decided by no more than a couple of shots. The same holds true in match play, where rules violations, inadvertent or not, frequently lead to a loss of the hole. And lots of those contests are lost by only that margin as well. Plus, there is the mental effect a violation and penalty can have. They can really rattle a golfer, and I have seen plenty of people go down in smoke after they have had to concede a hole or give up a stroke or two just because their ball moved at address, or they grounded their club in a hazard. Those kind of errors truly can be maddening.

Read on, then, and find out about some of the madness the rules of golf have wreaked. I describe ten (plus one) of the most devastating penalties I have ever heard of. No, I won't include those well-known disasters involving Craig Stadler, Paul Azinger, Pat Bradley, and Roberto de Vicenzo, because I mention them in other parts of the book. Instead, I offer you a whole new set of golf course breakdowns. Pay attention, because they *could* happen to you.

Bad Hands

A friend of mine was playing in a local tournament a couple of summers ago, and he had been hitting the ball well when he came up to the 14th green at a top area course and bent down to mark his ball. After slipping a coin underneath his Titleist, he tossed it over to his caddie for a routine cleaning. Now, the caddie was not quite ready for that, and he fumbled the ball, which then proceeded to roll off the putting surface, down a slope and into a small pond that was guarding the green. Neither of them could find the ball in the water, so my friend simply pulled another out of his pocket, put it where his mark was, made his two putts for par and moved on to the next tee. No problem, right?

Oh, but there was a big problem, and when an official caught up with him on the next hole, he explained that Rule 16-1b, under which the ball was lifted, does not permit substitution of another ball, no matter how the first one was lost. The result was a 2-stroke penalty, a missed cut by only 1 stroke and a lot of swearing at his caddie on what had to have been a very long car ride home. (And as I understand it, the caddie didn't help matters much by chastising his player for thinking he was Randy Johnson and saying, "If the ball had been thrown a little higher, I would have caught it.")

Bad Throw

A guy I was competing against one day got so angry with his round (as well he should have, given the way he was swinging the club that morning) that he took his ball, which had spun off the green of a hole we were playing, and hurled it into a nearby lake. After he composed himself, he put down a new ball on the spot where his original one had come to rest and finished up the hole. The club professional came by in a golf cart shortly afterward and made it clear that my opponent could not do that without incurring a penalty (under Rule 18-2a) that called for a loss of the hole. As it turned out, that was my margin of victory (because he started playing significantly better, and I tightened up). And I couldn't resist asking him how his throwing arm was the several times I saw him right after that match.

Bad Drop

South African touring professional John Bland took an improper drop at the 1999 PGA Senior Championship and got disqualified as a result. The calculated cost in terms of prize money he would have won had he not been booted out: $52,000.

Don't you think he spent a little time after that fiasco thinking about how he could have spent that money?

Bad Question

In the 1971 Ryder Cup matches in St. Louis, Arnold Palmer was playing Bernard Gallacher of Scotland when Palmer hit a great shot into a long par-3. Gallacher's caddie quickly complimented Palmer and asked, harmlessly, what club he had hit. The affable Arnie told him, and the group moved off the tee. But before the men had a chance to putt, a referee who had overheard the conversation awarded Palmer the hole because Gallacher's caddie had violated the rule (8-1) that, among other things, prohibits a caddy from asking advice of anyone other than the player he is carrying for. Arnold protested, but rules are rules, the referee said, and the decision had to stand.

Bad Agreement

Two fellows who were playing a match at their local club agreed at the start of play to concede all putts "within the leather," which meant any that were no longer than the space between their putter blade and grip. Questionable as that practice may be for friends who are hacking around a golf course on a weekend, it is definitely not something you do under any circumstances during a tournament, especially when you are talking about putts for the entire round (and not on a case-by-case basis). So when the players offhandedly told the club professional at the end of their round what they had done, he had no choice but to disqualify them both under Rule 1-3, which states that players may not agree to waive any rule or penalty. And by conceding the putts in advance, the players were violating Rule 2-4, which states that the only stroke that may be conceded in a match is the "next stroke".

Bad Club

A top amateur player was competing in his club championship when he and his caddie found a pitching wedge lying on the side of the 12th green of their course. The caddie looked at the name taped to the top of the shaft, recognized it as a member he often carried for, and without his golfer knowing it, put the club into his bag so he could return it to the pro shop at the end of the round. Everything was fine until the round was done, and the caddie pulled the extra club out at the pro shop and handed it to the guy working the bag room. One of the other competitors saw what had happened and called my friend for having too many clubs in his bag (Rule 4-4). The pro had no choice but to agree, however, and it cost the player four strokes, and ultimately, the championship.

Bad Decision

I was playing in a special media tournament during the Hassan II Trophy in Rabat, Morocco, a few years ago, and I missed a very easy putt on the second hole of the Blue Course at the deluxe Royal Dar Es Salaam golf club. Rather than finish up, I scooped up my ball with my putter and walked off the green, furious with myself and ready to move on to the next hole. I quickly hit my tee shot, and only then did I realize that I had made a big mistake. You see, I was competing in a stroke play event, not match play, and it was incumbent on me to hole out on every hole. By not completing the second hole before I put my ball into play on #3, I had violated Rule 3-2. And sadly, the penalty for that was disqualification.

So I was out of the tournament. But I did have a very good time at the black-tie ball I attended that evening.

Bad Practice

Another time I was playing in my club's big member-guest tournament, and my partner and I walked off the 16th tee after holing out and headed up to the 17th tee, which happens to be located at the far end of our practice range. Unfortunately, the group in front of us had not cleared the green at 17, which is a par-3, so my partner and I and our two opponents had to cool our heels for a spell. After lolling around the tee, my perpetually restless teammate walked over to the edge of the practice range, a mere ten yards away, and started hitting balls that had landed on the far reaches of the range back toward the teeing area. All he was doing was killing time, but our opponent said he was actually violating Rule 7-2, which deals with practicing during a round and says that although a player may chip or putt on or near the putting green of the hole last played, he is not allowed to hit a bunch of 5-irons. So we lost the next hole before we had even played it. (But goodness won out in the end, because we ended up winning the match.)

Bad Swing

Two women were playing in the first round of a single-elimination, best-ball tournament, and they were only one hole up on their opponents in what has been a very tightly-contested match. All four players hit their drives on the 17th hole, and all four balls ended up in the fairway. As often happens in events like this, there was a wait, and so the players were standing around chatting as the group ahead of them putted out. One of the women on 17 was actually half-swinging a 7-iron she planned to use for her approach shot as she talked when, lo and behold, she accidentally hit her ball, incurring a 1-stroke penalty in the process. That was all her opponents needed, and they were able to win that hole, and the match, as a result.

Bad Luck

During the 1946 U.S. Open, which was played at the Canterbury Golf Club outside Cleveland, Byron Nelson's caddie accidentally kicked his boss's ball on one hole, costing him a penalty stroke. And sure enough, it came back to haunt the smooth-swinging Texan as Nelson ended up tied with two other players at the end of regulation play and then lost in a playoff.

Bad Idea

A few summers ago, another good friend got a bit carried away during a party at his club's big member-guest tournament and ended up expressing his affection for his dinner partner at the end of the evening in much too public a manner. Only a handful of people actually saw what transpired between this much-chagrined man and his paramour, and no one in attendance seemed particularly offended (though everyone agreed it was perhaps the dumbest thing he had ever done). But news of his peccadillo spread through the club — and through the town — like a case of head lice, and eventually served to offend a number of high-minded people (none of whom, of course, had ever committed an indiscretion of their own). Full of moral indignation, they took swift action, and my friend was suspended from his club and thoroughly disgraced.

Now, that's what I call a devastating penalty. The only thing is, I'm still not sure which rule he violated.

Chapter 11

The Ten Best Games and Bets to Make in Golf

● ●

In This Chapter

▶ Getting some tips on betting

▶ Knowing which games are the most fun on the golf course

● ●

I have a good friend, Stephen Murray, who put the whole concept of gambling and golf into perspective for me one day when we were competing against each other in a club tournament. "I really don't care who wins this match," he said with a bright grin. "I just want to make sure I win the Nassau."

Now, to understand this story, you need to understand that Stephen is not some depraved handicapper who spends hours at the racetrack, has his college football bookie on speed dial, and likes hanging around strip joints when he has collected his winnings at the end of the day. He is, in fact, a well-spoken, well-educated, and well-mannered family man with a lovely wife, two terrific children, and no interest in ever betting on anything else in life. Not even bingo at the local church.

But a $4 Nassau, which is only one of many games you can play when you head out to the course, is something different altogether. And Stephen is like a lot of us who eschew gambling in every other form but find that a little action on the links makes a round of golf that much more enjoyable. Even if you're playing a tournament that with all reasonable expectation should be more important than the bet. And even if you end up losing a few bucks.

Notice, however, that Stephen and I are friends. And that I only said "a few bucks." Betting is fun, but my credo is that you only do it with people you know and trust, and you never make the wager so high that somebody gets upset at the end of the round. The most I have seen anyone lose in my regular games is $40, and that is with all sorts of junk going on and a few lucky birdies added in. Usually, the winners pocket anywhere from $5 to $10 apiece, and then we all go to the grill room for some refreshment before heading home.

Here are a few tips for betting in golf:

✔ **Always use handicaps when betting, and never let anyone talk you out of strokes that are rightfully yours.** If one of your opponents is a 6 handicap and you are a 10, you get 4 extra strokes for the 18-hole round. Those strokes will fall on what are generally regarded as the four hardest holes on the course, and they will no doubt come in very handy. (For example, if you, as a 10 handicap, get a 5 on one of those holes and your opponent, as a 6, gets a 4, then you tie, or halve, the hole because of your extra stroke. If, however, you both get 4s, you win because of the handicap situation.)

✔ **Don't ever give your opponents an extra stroke or two because they claim they haven't been playing very much.** Your handicap is your handicap, and if you're not willing to use the one you have, then don't play until you are.

In my usual group, we all know each other's handicap very well, so it is next to impossible for any of us to be fooled by another. And we trust each other well enough that if someone brings a newcomer into the mix, we are not inclined to ask a lot of questions about his handicap. But there are people better known as *sandbaggers,* who purposely keep their handicap high (by turning in only bad scores) and make good money by beating unsuspecting marks. As far as I am concerned, those types of golfers are nothing more than unrepentant cheats and should be tossed off the course when they are found out. And they are also the sort that you should never get into a match with because it will only serve to cost you a lot of money and aggravation.

✔ **Set up teams according to handicap.** Picking teams is part of the fun where I play. We argue and banter on the 1st tee, lying about how badly we have all been playing and how many strokes we should get from each other. We joke around long enough to create some semblance of animosity or tension between a few of the guys, and then we pair off based on who feels like going after whom. Or maybe one of the guys has an old score he wants to settle or simply wants to prove a point. We do that because we have all known each other for a while, and the verbal abuse that we dish out during a round is very much part of the process. And it all works for us because we have a fairly consistent weekend group.

But it is not always wise to throw a foursome together so haphazardly, especially if you have strangers involved. In most cases, the lowest and highest handicappers (the best and worst golfers in the foursome) should team up. That evens out the bet, and if everybody's handicap is about right, it will lead to the best competition.

✔ **Beware of strangers.** People often talk about never betting with a guy who has a 1-iron in his bag (because those clubs are almost impossible to hit, and anyone who carries one must be very good), a deep tan (because he, or she, has clearly been spending too much time out on the golf course), or a Southern accent (no offense here, but that scares a lot of us Yankees, because we figure you men and women from the South are able to get out on the course a lot more than we are up North and are therefore better players). And that's good advice. There are other things to notice, too, but the key is to make sure you know as much about your teammate — and your opponent — as is possible before you tee it up and start putting your children's college fund at risk.

The first-tee is one of the great spots in the world on a weekend morning, with the dew still on the fairway ahead, the sun low in the sky, the temperature not too warm, and four friends getting ready to play. This is where we decide the teams, figure out who is going first (usually by spinning a tee and having whomever it points to lead off), joke about what we did — or didn't do — the previous evening, and make the bet. There is usually a lot of chatter and a lot of laughs. But that's the point, isn't it? Now, on to the games you can play and bets you can place.

Nassau

The Nassau is the "Old Reliable" of golf bets, and the one you come across most often. Actually, a Nassau consists of three different bets — one for the front 9, another for the back 9, and a third for the entire 18 holes. You can even spice it up by *pressing the bet* whenever you get down by two holes or more, which means you are creating a new bet in the hopes of gaining back some of your money. Some people like automatic presses, but my friends and I never play that way. You don't want somebody to feel compelled to bet if he doesn't really want to. And if a person does not offer a press, that gives his opponents something to razz him about for the rest of the match. ("And you call yourself a man," someone may say. Or, "I can understand why you don't want to press. Two dollars really is a lot of money.")

Golf can be a very rough sport.

Most times, my friends and I play what is known as *2-2-4,* in which each nine is worth $2 and the 18-hole match $4. The team that wins the most holes on each nine and the full 18 wins those individual bets. Win all three, and you get $8. Win a couple of presses along the way, and you get more. (By the way, a press on one of the nines is worth the same amount as the regular bet of $2. And a press of the match is worth $4.)

I know some guys who prefer to play 5-5-10, which means the bets are worth $5, $5, and $10. And that's one of the beauties of a Nassau; you can play it for as little or as much money as you want.

A Nassau is a best-ball match, which means two-man teams are competing against each other, and the winner and loser for each hole is determined by which team has the best score. Only one score from a team is needed, so it doesn't matter if one golfer falters as long as the other plays well.

Nassaus, like all betting games, should be played at handicap, meaning that players with higher handicaps get strokes from those with lower handicaps. As I discuss in Chapter 8, that's how the playing field is kept level in golf. And it's also how things are kept fair.

Skins

Skins is the game you see the pros play on TV event each year, and it is very simple to learn. Each hole is worth a *skin,* and the value of that skin can range from $1 to $100, or even more. (My friends and I usually play dollar skins, or maybe $2. But any more is a little rich for our blood.) Whoever wins a hole, wins a skin, and you have carryovers if there is a tie. (And in skins, the rules are: one tie, all tie.) So, if the first hole is tied, the second hole is worth two skins. If that is tied as well, the third hole is worth three skins. And so forth.

Skins is a fun game, especially if you have only three players and not a foursome, for which Nassau is best-suited. But it can drive you crazy at times because a player who hasn't hit a decent ball all round can cash in with a lucky shot and win a bunch of money if it's a hole with a lot of carryovers. And that has happened to me more times than I care to remember.

Wolf

Wolf is one of my favorite games. In it, one player is designated the wolf on each hole and gets to pick the person he plays with based on the quality of his tee shot. To start, you set up a rotation at the first tee, deciding on which holes each person will be the wolf. The wolf always hits last, and after watching each person hit, has to decide whether he wants that person with him or not. If he doesn't like any of the drives he has seen, or if he's really ambitious, the wolf can decide to go it alone, which doubles the bet, usually $1 or $2 per hole, whether he wins or loses. The key is that the wolf has to decide after each drive and cannot have the luxury of seeing everybody hit first. The game is fun because it keeps mixing up the teams and changes the alliances with each hole, causing plenty of dissension and ribbing along the way. Keep track of who won which hole (both members of a team get a point if they win a hole, and ties are carried over), and then tally it all up at the end.

Points

Points is a very simple game that works when and if you're tired of the everyday Nassau. Each hole is worth six points. If everybody ties, then each player gets two points. If one guy wins, and another finishes second, they get four and two points respectively while the laggard gets stiffed. If two players tie, then each get three points. And in the end, whoever has the most points, again usually worth $1 or $2, wins the most money.

Dollar a Yard

Dollar a yard is popular up in Toronto and big among high-rolling businessmen everywhere. Win a 400-yard hole, and you put $400 on your side of the ledger. Some folks of more modest means have been known to play a dime or nickel a yard, or even a penny. But don't sneer at that penny bet; a 7,000-yard course can still be worth $70.

Pink Lady

In this game, a single pink golf ball is shared among a foursome and must be played by the person who lost the previous hole. The player stuck with the ball at the end of each nine holes is out a predetermined amount of money to each of the others.

Junk or Side Cheese

Every good golf match has what seasoned veterans call *junk bets* or *side cheese.* They are little contests outside the normal Nassau or skins match that bring a bit more money into the picture and a little more action onto the course. The most common forms of junk are greenies, sandies and birdies (with birdies paying double). To win a *greenie,* you have to hit your ball closest to the hole on a par-3 and make your par. To win a *sandy,* you have to make a par on a hole during which you have had to hit at least one shot out of a bunker. (And there are such things as *double sandies,* which occur if you end up in two different bunkers on a hole and still make your par. Sound impossible? Well, it's not, and I have done it several times myself.) Finally, to get a *birdie,* you actually have to make a birdie. Usually, the bets for junk are for $1, and they are handled on a team basis.

Some people like to get really creative with junk by adding *barkies* (parring a hole after hitting a tree), *roadies* (parring a hole after bouncing your ball off a road or cart path), *carties* (parring a hole after hitting someone's golf cart), and who knows what else. It all depends on what you can come up with.

Playing with the Pro

Playing with the pro is another good game for threesomes. Basically, you create an imaginary person for your fourth, give him a scratch handicap (meaning he gets no strokes at all), and call him the pro. And you rotate, each golfer playing six holes with the pro in what turns out to be an 18-hole Nassau, with the usual bets on the nines and junk. Of course, the pro always makes par in this best-ball match (but he can't make any greenies, sandies, or birdies, so he is useless as far as junk is concerned). And everybody in the group gets their strokes off of his scratch handicap.

Hog Press

Desperate times call for desperate measures, and the hog press is usually the act of a desperate team. What it is, quite simply, is a separate side bet, wagered on the last hole, by a team who is losing and wants one last chance at redemption. Generally, the amount put up in a hog press is higher than the agreed upon 18-hole bet, and it is something completely different from anything else that may still be active. The person who wins the last hole wins the hog, and all the glory — and money — that comes with it.

The Big Hawaiian

This bet is somewhat akin to the hog in that it is not proffered until the last hole. But the difference with the Big Hawaiian is that it is essentially a double-or-nothing proposition, again put up by the team getting its brains beaten out. Say you and your partner are down $10 each as you head to the 18th tee. Suggest the Big Hawaiian, and you owe nothing if you win 18. You still owe $10 if you halve the hole, and you drop $20 apiece if the bad guys come out on top.

The Big Hawaiian drives the people in the lead crazy because they do not want 17 good holes of work to go down the drain with one lousy bet. To them, it is an inherently sleazy move on the part of the losing team and usually treated with great disdain. But to pass on the Big Hawaiian is to open yourself up to endless criticism for copping out and showing, in the minds of your opponents, a complete lack of courage, adventure, and fun. So even though a bet like that goes against most every golfer's better judgment when they get to the 18th hole with a lead, they know in their hearts that they have to take it if they want to be able to walk around the course in the future with any sort of dignity. The Big Hawaiian can cause enormous anxiety; nothing is quite so delicious as watching your opponent's $20 lead evaporate in one lucky shot.

The greatest Big Hawaiian player of all-time is George Rippey of Fairfield, Connecticut, who can sleepwalk through 17 holes and then pull off the most magical of shots on the 18th. The man has put his kids through college with the money he has earned — and saved — by winning Big Hawaiians, and driven his usual playing partners (Bruds, Crazy, and Scottso) to drink and other insidious vices. You don't want to bet against George in that situation, and nothing strikes greater fear in a player's heart at my place than the Ripper exclaiming as he walks of the 17th green, "I can hear Don Ho singing."

Chapter 12

Ten Things You Can Learn about Golf Rules and Etiquette from the Movies

• •

In This Chapter

▶ Taking tips from the movies on the rules of golf

▶ Avoiding the mistakes made by your favorite film characters

• •

*M*ovies can't tell us much about how to swing a golf club properly. Witness Matt Damon's feeble hacks in *The Legend of Baggar Vance.* And Kevin Costner's driving range buddy, Earl, sure got it right in *Tin Cup* when he watched Renee Russo take a couple of shots with her driver before saying, "How does such a pretty girl have such an ugly swing?" In fact, the same question could have been asked of Cameron Diaz in *There's Something About Mary.*

However, when it comes to rules and etiquette, Hollywood can teach us a few things about golf. Mostly, it is about how *not* to act on the course. But at least the moviemakers get that much right.

When You Hit into the Water, Drop a New Ball Where the First One Entered the Hazard

The agonizingly ridiculous final scene of *Tin Cup,* in which Roy "Tin Cup" McAvoy keeps dumping 3-woods into the pond guarding the par-five 18th green, provides a valuable lesson as to how to deal with a ball that you have just powered into the drink. No, it is not necessary to keep flailing away from the spot where the original shot was played. Instead, you are allowed under the rules (26-1) to go up to where the ball entered the water hazard and drop a new one. And that is what Costner's character does in the first three rounds of that fictional U.S. Open, before losing his mind completely on the fourth and final day. And he's able to make par every time.

Never Land a Helicopter While Players Are Teeing Off

You can pick up a key bit of etiquette from *M*A*S*H:* Never, ever land a helicopter on an area where golfers are in the process of teeing off. Especially when they are "the pros from Dover." It is very, very bad form.

Avoid Thunderstorms

Caddyshack provides a critical bit of information about playing in bad weather. And that is: Never tee it up in a thunderstorm, even if the heavy stuff is not going to come down for a while. After all, look what it did to the Bishop.

Watch Where You Hit Your Ball

In *Animal House,* Otter and Boon clearly have a love of the game of golf as they tee up shots and spray them all over the campus of Faber College. But they could use a lesson or two on basic etiquette. It is not, for example, a good idea to hit a ball into the school cafeteria kitchen, hit a ball through the window of Dean Wormer's office and shatter his water pitcher, or hit a ball into the flank of a very skittish white horse. Well, considering the neo-Nazi who was riding the horse at the time, maybe that wasn't such a bad move after all.

Keep Your Eye on Your Ball — and Your Caddy

In the movie *Goldfinger,* the players are James Bond and Auric Goldfinger. The setting is the Stoke Park Club north of London. And the stakes are a solid gold bar (worth approximately $12,000 at the time) or the cash equivalent. The match is even after 16 holes, and after Bond hits a good drive on 17, Goldfinger yanks his drive into the left rough. Five minutes are almost up (the maximum time allowed to search for a ball before it is considered lost) when Goldfinger's caddie

Oddjob drops a new one down his pant leg for his boss. That ball is a Slazenger 1, the same kind Goldfinger had teed off with, and he hopes Bond won't notice. But just as Goldfinger says he has found his original ball, the British agent actually stumbles upon the real one himself. Instead of telling his nemesis, who has a penchant for breaking the rules in any game he plays, 007 pockets the ball. He also finds another Slazenger in the rough, this one a #7, and he decides to take that as well so he can have a little fun with Goldfinger.

007 lets the arch villain play out 17, which they halve. And when he picks Goldfinger's ball out of the cup on that green, he switches the #1 with the #7. When Goldfinger tees off with that ball on 18, Bond has him just where he wants him, because it is against the rules (15-2) to play the wrong ball, and if it happens in match play, you lose the hole. He calls Goldfinger on that move on the 18th green, and the man loses the hole and the $12,000 (which was a lot of money back when this movie was made).

The moral of the story? Always make sure you are playing your own ball before you hit. And keep your eye on your opponent's caddie so he doesn't try to do the same thing Oddjob did.

Know Where to Drop

In *Caddyshack,* Chevy Chase asks for a ruling as he is practicing the night before his big match when his ball comes to rest in a coffee cake tin in the assistant greenskeeper's hovel. And Bill Murray gives it to him, in between swigs of cheap wine: You may take a drop — and a 1-stroke penalty — when you have an unplayable lie.

Don't Take Advice from Anyone Other Than Your Caddy

In *Tin Cup,* Roy McAvoy is trying to qualify for the U.S. Open, and he has just finished a blistering front nine. So he's feeling very comfortable and confident on the 10th tee and ready to take out the Big Dog (his driver) and draw his tee shot over some trees. His caddy, Romeo, disagrees with the strategy, and the two start to argue. Furious, McAvoy, played by Costner, turns to his shrink/love interest Renee Russo and asks what he should hit, the driver or an iron. But before she can answer, a man in the gallery reminds the golfer that soliciting advice from someone other than his caddie is a 2-stroke penalty (Rule 8-1). And he's right.

But that setback doesn't seem to bother "Tin Cup." Nor does the fact that he and his caddie get so exercised with each other on that tee that they proceed to break all but one of Costner's clubs. He manages to par his whole way in with a 7-iron, make it to the Open and, of course, get the girl. (This is, after all, Hollywood.)

Keep It Moving

In *Caddyshack,* the importance of keeping pace on the course is apparent. Slow play is the bane of most golf clubs, and it certainly frustrated Tony the caddy when he had the Havercamp couple out in *Caddyshack.* What more could his buddies in the caddy pen say when he returned from a seemingly interminable loop but, "What'd they do, die on you, Tony?"

Don't make anyone feel like they are dying on the course (unless, of course, it's your opponent, and the reason he is feeling so sick is that you are really putting it to him). There's no reason a round should run any longer than four and a half hours for a foursome.

Be Silent When Other Golfers Are Hitting the Ball

In *Caddyshack,* Danny Noonan (Michael O'Keefe) is getting ready to knock in a tough putt to win the caddie championship at the Bushwood Country Club, but he's not getting any respect from his opponent and some of the gallery. "Miss it, Noonan," they bark as he stands over his ball. "Miss it, Noonan," they holler as he starts his stroke. "Miss it, Noonan," they yell as it rolls toward the cup.

There's no excuse for this sort of behavior, and golfers should always be silent when their opponents — and their partners — are playing. Few things in the sport are worse than one player talking during another's swing.

By the way, Danny sunk his putt, won the trophy (which was about the size of a candy bar and could not have cost more than a couple of bucks), and later that same day he, too, got the girl.

Always Pay What You Owe

One of the final scenes in *Caddyshack* is when Rodney Dangerfield's obnoxious character confronts the Judge (played by Ted Knight) and demands that he pay the $80,000 in bets he had just lost to him. Of

course, Knight refuses. So Rodney turns to a pair of rather burly gentlemen and says, "Hey, Moose. Rocko. Help the judge find his wallet."
They immediately take after Knight, and we get another important
lesson in the process. Always pay off your wagers before you leave the
course. I have known people over the years who regularly stiffed their
playing opponents, and it is simply bad manners. No, it's not up there
with cheating, but it is close.

Part V
Appendixes

"What exactly do the rules say about giving and receiving advice?"

In this part . . .

The appendixes in this part are great places to turn for more information. Here you'll find a glossary of golf terms to help you out when talk of the game makes you feel like you're listening to another language. And I give you a great resource section that provides contact information, including Web sites, for places that can help make the game even better.

Appendix A

Glossary

N
o, you won't get any foreign language credit for studying and learning the following words and terms. But you will have a better understanding of how golfers talk about rules, etiquette, and the game itself.

addressing the ball: A player has addressed the ball when he has taken his stance and has also grounded his club, except that in a hazard, a player has only to take his stance to address the ball (because he may not ground his club there).

advice: Any counsel or suggestion that could influence a player's decision regarding his club selection, how he plays a hole, and the way he makes a stroke. The term does not refer to questions regarding rules or matters of public information, such as the position of hazards or the flagstick on putting greens.

albatross: See *double eagle.*

approach: A shot to the green from anywhere but the tee.

away: Term used to describe the ball farthest from the hole, and therefore the one to be played next.

back nine: The second half of an 18-hole course.

ball at rest: A ball that is not moving.

ball in play: A ball is "in play" as soon as the player has made a stroke on the tee, and it remains that way until it is holed out on the green. Except, of course, when it is lost, hit out-of-bounds, or substituted with another ball.

best ball: Used in a variety of games involving four players facing off as two teams of two. The low score on each team (the best ball) counts as the team score.

birdie: Score of one stroke under par on a hole. Birdies are good.

bogey: Score of one stroke over par on a hole. For many players, especially the pros, bogeys are bad.

bunker: A hazard filled with sand.

caddie: The person carrying your clubs during a round of golf. A good caddie will also dispense yardage, read greens, proffer sage advice, and keep you from becoming an emotional wreck during particularly tense times. Take caddies whenever possible and pay them generously if they perform well.

casual water: Water on the course that is visible before or after a player takes his stance but is not a water hazard. You may lift your ball from casual water without penalty.

concede: To give an opponent a putt, hole, or match.

divot: The piece (or pieces) of turf displaced by the club head during a swing. Some divots are so big that they look as large as those wigs worn by judges in England or possibly the fur of a beaver that has been skinned. And for that reason, we sometimes call those divots *pelts*.

dogleg: A hole where the fairway curves one way or the other, like a dog's leg.

double bogey: Score of two strokes over par on a hole. Very bad.

double eagle: Score of three under par on a hole. Also known as an *albatross*. Very good, and almost impossible to get.

drop: The procedure by which you put your ball back into play after it's been deemed unplayable.

eagle: Score of two under par for a hole. Fantastic.

embedded ball: A ball that is either fully or partially embedded in the ground.

fairway: The closely mowed surface running from the tee to the green. Where you want your drives to go.

foot wedge: A way to describe a foot that covertly — and conveniently — kicks a ball out of a bad position for a player. Only cheaters use foot wedges.

free drop: A drop for which no penalty is incurred (and no price is charged).

front nine: The first half of an 18-hole golf course.

gallery: Spectators at a tournament.

gimme: A short putt that you give your opponent, or your opponent gives you, because it seems almost impossible to miss.

green: The shortest-cut grass where you do your putting.

greenie: A bet among players over the closest ball to the pin on a par-3; the winner must not only be on the green but also make at least par on the hole.

ground the club: When you place your club head behind your ball at address, usually touching the ground in the process.

ground under repair: An area on a golf course being worked on by the maintenance crew, generally marked by white lines. You may drop your ball from those spots without penalty.

handicap: A number you get through a system developed by the United States Golf Association that basically rates your ability as a player relative to par. The handicap system allows golfers of all abilities to play together by giving players with high handicaps strokes from those who have lower ones.

hazard: Either a bunker or a water hazard. *Remember:* You cannot ground your club in a hazard.

hole out: When you complete play on a hole.

honor: The player who is to play first from the tee is said to have the honor. And the person, or team, that records the lowest score on the previous hole has the honor.

impact: The moment at which the club head strikes the ball.

in your pocket (IP): What you do when you decide not to finish a hole and pick up your ball. Usually, the end result of several bad swings.

lateral water hazard: Any water hazard marked by red stakes and usually parallel to the fairway.

lie: Where your ball is on the ground. Sometimes, it is sitting up nicely, and that is called a *good lie*. But if your ball is stuck in a divot or buried in very thick rough, then that constitutes a *bad lie*. (And no, you may not kick it out.)

lift: What you do with your ball before you drop.

loose impediment: Natural debris such as stones, leaves, twigs, branches, worms, and bugs that you can remove from around your ball as long as the ball does not move.

lost ball: A ball that cannot be found.

mark: What you do to indicate the position of your ball, usually on the green, so that it is not in the way of other golfers.

marker: What you use to mark your ball, usually a coin or some other small, round, and flat object. Also, a person who keeps a competitor's score.

match play: A golf game played between two sides. The side that wins the most holes wins the match.

medal play: Also called *stroke play,* this is a game among any number of players, with the one posting the lowest aggregate score winning.

municipal course: A course owned by the local government and open to the public. Usually, the fees for such layouts are lower, and so are the standards for course maintenance at them.

Nassau: A bet in which the round of 18 holes is divided into three matches: the front 9, the back 9, and the full 18.

out of bounds (OB): The area beyond the boundaries of the course, usually marked with white stakes. This is where really bad shots go. A player who has hit out of bounds has to play another ball from the original spot, taking a one-stroke penalty in the process. Ouch!

par: The score a good player should make on a hole or for a round.

preferred lies: When you can move your ball to a more favorable position as a result of water or some other condition that makes the fairways difficult to play. Sometimes, local rules allow for that.

press: A new bet, put forth by a player or team who is losing their match, in the hopes of gaining back some of their money.

private club: A club open only to members and their guests.

pro-am: A competition in which professional golfers team up with one or more amateurs. Very expensive in many cases, and very fun.

provisional ball: A timesaving maneuver in which a ball is played when the original one is feared to be lost. If the first ball is indeed lost, then the second one is in play.

relief: What you take when you drop a ball that was in a hazard or affected by an obstruction.

rough: The areas of long grass outside the fairways, tees, and greens that is difficult to hit out of. Where you want your opponent's drives to end up.

sandy: A bet for making par after being in a bunker. If you are able to make par after being in two bunkers, you get a double sandy.

scratch player: A person with a 0 handicap; someone who is expected to shoot par.

semi-private club: A club that has members but that is also open to the general public.

spike mark: What players with spiked golf shoes often leave on the green. *Remember:* Spike marks may not be repaired if they are in the way of your putt.

stance: A player takes his stance when he places his feet in position to make a swing.

stroke: Movement of the club with intent to hit the ball. A player who checks his downswing voluntarily before the club head reaches the ball has not made a stroke.

stroke hole: A hole where a player either gets or gives a stroke based on the handicaps being used in that match.

stroke play: See *medal play.*

teeing ground: The area where you tee up your ball and from which you hit your drive. Tee markers tell you where you must hit your drive from, and you may not go forward of them. You may, however, tee your ball up as many as two clubs lengths behind the markers.

triple bogey: Three over par on a hole, and a very ugly number.

unplayable lie: A lie from which it is impossible to play your ball. You get a drop, but that comes with a penalty stroke as well.

water hazard: Any sea, lake, pond, river, or ditch marked by yellow stakes. Hit your ball in there, and it will cost you a shot, and usually the ball itself.

Appendix B

Resources

● ●

Web Sites

*T*here is so much great golf information to be found on the Internet these days, and the sites listed in this section are some of the best out there, especially as they relate to golf news, rules, travel, and equipment. No, they don't offer anything that is nearly as good as actually playing the game. But there is still plenty of interesting material. So log on, and have yourself some fun.

Rules

The only two sites you need to know for information on rules are those run by the two governing bodies of golf, the United States Golf Association (www.usga.org) and the Royal & Ancient Golf Club of St. Andrews (www.randa.org).

News

I am unabashedly prejudiced about the site of *Golfweek,* the magazine I work for (www.golfweek.com), but that is not the only reason I recommend it above all others in this category. It truly is the best, and I urge anyone looking for news and information on professional golf tours, top amateur players and events, important issues, personality profiles, and golf business to check it out.

Other news-related sites you may want to visit include the one for *Golf Digest* and *Golf World* magazines (www.golfdigest.com); *Golf* magazine (golfonline.com); *Sports Illustrated* (www.sportsillustrated. cnn.com); ESPN (espn.go.com); and the Golf Channel (www.thegolfchannel.com).

Travel

A number of travel-related sites are available on the Internet, and if you are thinking about taking your game on the road, you may want to go to the following:

- ✔ Global Golf: www.globalgolf.com
- ✔ GolfCourse.com, *Golf* magazine's course guide: www.golfcourse.com
- ✔ InterGolf, a terrific high-end tour operation: www.intergolfvacations.com
- ✔ PerryGolf, another top tour operator: www.perrygolf.com
- ✔ Wide World of Golf: www.wideworldgolf.com
- ✔ World Golf: www.worldgolf.com

Courses

Several of the best-known golf courses and/or resorts have their own sites, including Pebble Beach (www.pebblebeach.com); PGA West (www.pgawest.com); Pinehurst (www.pinehurst.com); and St. Andrews (www.standrews.com).

Shopping

As a matter of etiquette for private club members, I have always thought it important that they buy their golf equipment from their club professionals. If you don't belong to a club, however, you have a number of other places to get your balls, shoes, and clubs, even on the Internet.

Three of the best places are Edwin Watts (www.edwinwatts.com); Golfsmith (www.golfsmith.com); and Golf Galaxy (www.golfgalaxy.com). These are big golf retail outlets, and they have excellent service, prices, and selections.

Miscellaneous

You can also find a variety of general golf Web sites that cover everything from the tours, instruction, and handicap information to shopping, rules, and trivia. Perhaps the best ones are:

- ✔ Nothing But Golf: www.nothingbutgolf.com
- ✔ GolfServ: www.golfserv.com
- ✔ Golfballs.com: www.golfballs.com

Golf Associations

In this section, I provide you with a list of golf associations around the world. If you're interested in finding the regional or sectional associations within your area of the United States, visit the PGA Web site (www.pga.com/sections/index.html) or the USGA Web site (www.usga.org/associations/index.asp). Or you can call the organizations' national headquarters; the information is listed in the following section.

North America

American Junior Golf Association (AJGA)
1980 Sports Club Drive
Braselton, GA 30514
Phone: 770-868-4200
Web site: www.ajga.org

American Society of Golf Course Architects
221 North LaSalle Street #3500
Chicago, IL 60611
Phone: 312-372-7090
Web site: www.golfdesign.org

Ladies Professional Golf Association (LPGA)
100 International Golf Drive
Daytona Beach, FL 32124-1092
Phone: 904-274-6200
Web site: www.lpga.com

Multicultural Golf Association of America (formerly Minority Golf Association of America)
P.O. Box 587
Glenn Dale, MD 20769
Phone: 631-288-8255
Web site: www.mgaa.com

National Association of Left-Handed Golfers
3249 Hazelwood Drive SW
Atlanta, GA 30311
Phone: 800-733-6006 (toll-free) or 561-744-6006
Web site: www.ngf.org

National Golf Foundation
1150 South U.S. Highway One
Suite 401
Jupiter, FL 33477
Phone: 800-733-6006 (toll-free) or 561-744-6006
Fax: 561-744-6107
E-mail: ngf@ngf.org
Web site: www.ngf.org

Professional Golfers' Association of America (PGA)
100 Avenue of the Champions
Box 109601
Palm Beach Gardens, FL 33410-9601
Phone: 561-624-8400
Web site: www.pga.com

Royal Canadian Golf Association
1333 Dorval Drive
Oakville, ON L6J 4Z3
Canada
Phone: 905-849-9700
Web site: www.rcga.org

United States Blind Golf Association
3094 Shamrock Street North
Tallahassee, FL 32308-2735
Phone/Fax: 850-893-4511
E-mail: usbga@blindgolf.com
Web site: www.blindgolf.com

United States Golf Association (USGA)
P.O. Box 708
1 Liberty Corner Road
Far Hills, NJ 07931
Phone: 908-234-2300
Web site: www.usga.org

Australia

Australian Golf Union (AGU)
Golf Australia House
155 Cecil Street
South Melbourne, Victoria 3205
Australia
Phone: 613-699-7944
Fax: 613-690-8510
Web site: 203.32.162.228/home/default.sps

Belgium

Royal Belgian Golf Federation
Chaussee de la Hulpe, 110
1050 Brussels
Belgium
Phone: 32 2 672 23 89
Fax: 32 2 672 08 97
Web site: www.frbg.be

Bermuda

Bermuda Golf Association
P. O. Box HM 433
Hamilton 5
Bermuda
Phone: 809 238-1367

Chile

Federacion Chilena de Golf
Av. El Golf 266
Santiago
Chile
Phone: (56-2) 362 0777
Fax: (56-2) 362 0929
Web site: www.chilegolf.cl

Costa Rica

National Golf Association of Costa Rica
PO Box 10969-1000
Av. 1, Calle 24-28
San Jose
Costa Rica
Phone: (506) 221-8120
Web site: www.edenia.com/anagolf

England

Golf Society of Great Britain
Hope Point
Granville Road
St Margarets Bay
Dover
Kent
CT15 6DT
England
Phone: 01304 852229

Finland

Finnish Golf Union
Radiokatu 20
PL 27, SF-00241 Helsinki
Finland
Phone: 3481 2590
Fax: 147 145
Web site: www.suomengolflehti.fi

France

French Golf Federation
68, rue Anatole France
92309 Levallois-Perret Cedex
France
Phone: 01.41.49.77.00
Fax: 01.41.49.77.01
Web site: www.ffg.org

Germany

Deutscher Golf Verband e.V.
Viktoriastr. 16
65189 Wiesbaden
Postfach 21 06
65011 Wiesbaden
Germany
Phone: 06 11 - 990 20 0
Fax: 06 11 - 990 20 40
Web site: www.golf.de/_dgv

Hong Kong

The Golf Association of Hong Kong, Ltd.
Suite 2003, Sports House, 1, Stadium Path,
So Kon Po, Causeway Bay
Hong Kong
Phone: 852-25228804
Fax: 852-28451553
Web site: www.hkga.com

Iceland

Golf Union of Iceland
Sport Center
104 Reykjavik
Iceland
Phone: 354-1-686686
Fax: 354-1-686086

Ireland

Golfing Union of Ireland
The Golfing Union of Ireland
81 Eglinton Road
Donnybrook, Dublin 4
Phone: (353) 1 2694111
Fax: (353) 1 2695368
Web site: www.gui.ie

India

The Indian Golf Union
Sukh Sagar, 2nd Floor
2/5 Sarat Bose Road
Calcutta
India 700 020

Jamaica

Jamaica Golf Association
c/o Constant Spring Golf Club
P.O. Box 743
Kingston 8
Jamaica
Phone: 876 925-2325
Fax: 876 924-6330

Japan

Japan Golf Association
606-6th Floor, Palace Building
Marunouchi, Chiyoda-ku
Tokyo, Japan
Phone: 813-215-0003
Fax: 813-214-2831

Korea

Korea Golf Association
18, 13 Floor Manhattan Bldg.
36-2 Yeo Eui Do-Dongan
Yeong, Deung Po-Ku
Seoul
Korea
Phone: 783-4748
Web site: www.kgagolf.or.kr

Malaysia

Malaysian Golf Association
No. 12-A Persiaran Ampang
55000 Kuala Lumpur
Malaysia
Phone: 60 3 4577931
Fax: 60 3 4565596

Mexico

Federacion Mexicana De Golf, A.C.
Av. Lomas De Sotelo 1112, Desp. 103
Col. Lomas De Sotelo
Mexico D.F, Mexico C.P. 11200
Phone: (52-5) 395-32-45
Fax: (52-5) 580-22-63
Web site: www.mexgolf.org

Morocco

Federation Royale Marocaine de Golf
Royal Golf Rabat dar es Salam
Route des Zaers
Rabat Moroccco
Phone: (07) 75 58 64/65
Fax: (07) 75 76 71

Netherlands

Netherlands Golf Federation
PO Box 221
3454 ZL De Meern
The Netherlands
Phone: 03406-21888
Fax: 03406-21177
Web site: www.golfsite.nl

New Zealand

New Zealand Golf Association
NZGA, Level 1, Xacta Tower
94 Dixon Street
P O Box 11842
Wellington, New Zealand
Phone: 04 385-4330
Fax: 04 385-4331
Web site: nzga.co.nz

Norway

Norwegian Golf Federation
Hauger Skolevei 1
1351 Rud
Oslo
Norway
Phone: 47-67-154600
Fax: 47-67-138640

Peru

Federacion Peruana de Golf
Estadio Nacional
Puerta 4, Piso 4
Peru
Phone: 5114-336515
Fax: 5114-338267

Philippines

Republic of the Philippines Golf Association
Roxas Blvd.
Makati
Philippines
Phone: 63 (2) 58-88-45
Fax: 63 (2) 521-1587

Republic of China

Golf Association of the Republic of China
12/F-1, 125 Nanking East Road Section 2
Taipei, Taiwan 104 ROC
Phone: 886-2-25165611
Fax: 886-2-25163208
Web site: www.proqc.com/~rocgolf/ga/garoc.html

Scotland

Royal and Ancient Golf Club of St. Andrews
Fife, KY16 9JD
Scotland
Phone: 01334 472112
Fax: 01334 477580
Web site: www.randa.org

Scottish Golf Union
Scottish National Golf Centre
Drumoig
Leuchars
St Andrews
Fife, KY16 0DW
Scotland
Phone: 01382 549500
Fax: 01382 549510
Web site: www.scottishgolf.com/sgu/

Singapore

Singapore Golf Association
PO Box 457
Singapore 912416
Phone: 65 466 4892
Fax: 65 486 4897

South Africa

South African Golf Federation
P.O. Box 391994
Bramley 2018
c/o Wanderers Club
Ielovo, Johannesburg, South Africa
Phone: 27 11 442 3723
Fax: 27 11 442 3753

Spain

Real Federación Española de Golf
Capitán Haya, 9 5
28020 Madrid
Spain
Phone: (91) 5552682-5552757
Fax: (91) 5563290
Web site: rfeg.sportec.es/rfeg/main.htm

Sweden

Swedish Golf Federation
Box 84
182 11 Daneryd
Sweden
Phone: 46-8622-1500
Fax: 46-8755-8439
Web site: sgf.golf.se/

Switzerland

Association Suisse de Golf
Place de la Croix Blanche 19
1066 Epalinges
Lausanne
Switzerland
Phone: 41-21-784-35-32
Fax: 41-21-784-35-91
Web site: www.ega-golf.ch

Thailand

Thailand Golf Association
83 Amnuay Songkram Road
Dusit
Bangkok 10300
Thailand
Phone: 662-537-8172
Fax: 662-537-8173

United Kingdom

European Golf Industry Association
Federation House
National Agricultural Centre
Stoneleigh Park
Warwickshire
CV8 2RF
England
Phone: 01203 417141
Fax: 01203 414990
E-Mail: egia'ortslife.co.uk
Web site: www.egia.org.uk

Venezuela

Federacion Venezolana de Golf
Unidad Comercial "La Florida"
Piso 1. Ofic. 8, Av.
Caracas, Venezuela 1050
Phone: (582) 731-7662
Fax: (582) 730-1660 / 730.2731
Web site: www.fvg.org

Wales

Welsh Golfing Union
Catshash
Gwent NP6 1JQ
Newport NP6 1JQ
Wales
Phone: 44-1633-430830
Fax: 44-1633-430843

Zimbabwe

Zimbabwe Golf Association
PO Box 3327
Harare
Zimbabwe

Index

• *Numbers* •

2-2-4 Nassau, 127
5-5-10 Nassau, 127

• *A* •

Achuhnet Company, 22
acknowledging well-played shot, 61
addressing ball
  putting green, 38
  talking and, 56
  tournament play, 108
advice
  asking, 37, 50, 135
  caddie asking, 121
  giving, 37, 59, 89, 90
"all square," 34
anger, 59, 62
Animal House, 134
Arizona Mid-Amateur of 2000, 20, 30
associations
  international, 150–151, 153–155, 158
  North America, 149–150
AT&T Pebble Beach National
    Pro-Am, 106
Atkinson, Craig, 61
audience for book, 2
Augusta National, 4, 111–112
Australian Golf Union, 150
author, qualifications of, 3–4
autographs
  asking for, 111
  locations for, 114
  pro-ams and, 105
  shoving items at players, 115
  times for, 115
Azinger, Paul, 20, 31

• *B* •

Baker-Finch, Ian, 32
ball
  addressing, 38, 108
  deflection or stopping of, 19
  driving range, 80
  dropping new where first entered
    hazard, 133
  hitting accidentally, 122
  improper drop, 120
  keeping handy, 58
  kicking accidentally, 123
  lifting, 39
  lost, 44–45, 59, 89
  out of bounds, 45
  overhanging hole, 40
  playing as it lay, 10, 38
  playing own, 18, 135
  playing same, 18, 34
  playing stroke while other in
    motion, 40
  provisional, 46
  putting green and, 83
  size of, 12, 17
  substituting, 120
  time limit to search for, 134
  unfit for play, 35–36
  unplayable, 19, 47, 135
  watching, 59
Ballesteros, Seve, 82
Bandon Dunes, 69
barkies, 130
Belgian golf association, 151
Bermuda Golf Association, 151
betting
  agreeing on, 60
  Big Hawaiian, 130–131
  caddie and, 71
  caution when, 125
  Dollar a Yard, 129
  handicap and, 126
  Hog Press, 130

betting *(continued)*
  junk bets or side cheese, 129
  municipal courses, 74
  Nassau, 127–128
  overview of, 94–95
  paying debts, 136
  Pink Lady, 129
  playing with the pro, 130
  Points, 129
  practice facility games, 85
  Skins, 128
  tips for, 126–127
  Wolf, 128
Big Hawaiian, 130–131
birdie, 129
Bland, John, 120
Bob Hope Chrysler Classic, 106
Bolt, Tommy, 63
boss, playing golf with, 92
Boulders, The, 69
British Open, 14
bunker
  ball lost, 44
  relief from immovable
    obstructions, 43
  unplayable ball, 48
business
  golf and, 3, 87
  golf school for executives, 97
business-related golf outings
  betting, 94–95
  boss, playing with, 92
  cell phone, 97
  clients, playing with, 87–92
  coworkers, playing with, 91
  drinking, 95
  observing person during, 93
  overview of, 101–103
  telling jokes, 95
  winning, 94

• *C* •

caddie
  advice from, 135
  asking advice, 121
  betting and, 71
  line of play and, 37
  number of, 20, 30

playing with, 66, 69–70
pro-ams and, 105
programs for, 67, 69
role of, 66–67
scholarship funds, 68
treatment of, 2
trends in use of, 68–69
working with, 77
Caddyshack, 1, 134–136
Callahan, Tom, 81
Callaway Golf, 21–23, 29
camera at tournament, 110
Canada, 13
Cantwell, Joseph, 16, 28
carties, 130
Casper, Billy, 96
celebrity golf outings, 103
cell phone
  business round, 97
  etiquette for, 1–2
  private club, 76
  tournament play, 109
charity-related golf outings, 103–104
cheating. *See also* self-policing
  business-related golf, 91
  golf compared to other sports, 26–27
  nonconforming club and, 23
  rules and, 16
checking in, 59
children and putting green, 84
Chilean golf association, 151
Chinese golf association, 155
chipping around putting green, 83
client, playing golf with, 87–92
clubs
  breaking, 63
  declaring out of play, 35
  design and manufacture of, 12, 20–23
  number of, 29, 35, 121
  selection and addition of, 35
  sharing, 35
  steel shaft, 17
  throwing, 59, 62–63
  use of own, 21
coefficient of resolution, 21
common sense and rules, 30–31
competitiveness, 94
complaining, 60
complimenting client, 88

conceding stroke, 121
Costa Rican golf association, 151
"country-club-for-a-day" courses
  dress code, 75
  overview of, 75
course Web sites, 148
courses. *See* municipal courses;
    private courses
coworker, playing golf with, 91
Curtis Cup, 15

• *D* •

Daly, John, 113
de Vicenzo, Roberto, 50
Decisions of the Rules of Golf, The, 33
DeRose, Diane, 90
devotion
  to game, 25–26
  to rules, 28, 29, 30
disqualification, 119
divots, replacing, 2, 56
Dollar a Yard, 129
Doral tournament of 1996, 19
dormie, 34
dress code
  business-related outing, 102
  "country-club-for-a-day" courses, 75
  informing partner of, 88
  municipal courses, 74
  private courses, 77–78
drinking. *See* liquor
drivers, titanium, 12, 17, 21–23, 29
driving range
  aim, watching, 80
  balls, leaving, 80
  balls, paying for, 80
  best moment on, 82
  hitting between ropes, 81
  line on, 80
  movies and, 81
  overview of, 79
  staying off, 82
dropping ball
  water hazard, 45
  when unplayable, 48
Druga, Jack, 29, 64, 102
Duval, David, 110, 113

• *E* •

East Lake Golf Club, 68
Edsell, G. L., 51
Eisenhower, Dwight, 71
Electrolux USA Championship, 106
English Amateur Championship of
    1979, 19
ERC (Callaway Golf), 22, 29
etiquette
  do's and don'ts, 56–60
  overview of, 55–56
European countries, certification in, 2
Evans, Chick, 68
executives, golf school for, 97
extreme conditions, 25

• *F* •

failure to hole out, 34
fans
  Augusta National, 111–112
  autograph seeking, 111, 114–115
  behavior of, 107
  best-behaved, 112
  calling network to report rules
      violations, 31–32
  cell phone and camera, 109–111
  Phoenix Open, 113
  running, 109
  tournaments and, 107–108, 110–113
  worst-behaved, 113
Finnish Golf Union, 151
flagstick, 41
foot wedge, 91
Foote, Nat, 62, 89
"Fore!," 56
Francis Ouimet Scholarship Fund, 68
French Golf Federation, 152

• *G* •

Gallacher, Bernard, 121
game, description of, 34
gamesmanship, 63–64
Gentlemen Golfers of Leith, The, 9, 11,
    14, 17

German golf association, 152
gift, exchanging, 103
Gill, Vince, 106
"gimme" putt, 93
Gladding, Reg, 19
Goldfinger, 134
golf
    as game of rules and etiquette, 2–3
    history of, 11–13
    other sports compared to, 26–28
Golfweek magazine, 3, 147
Graham, Tom, 28
Grant, Amy, 106
gratuities at private courses, 77
Great Britain, 51
greenie, 129
group
    holding up, 57
    walking ahead of, 56
group in front
    hitting and, 56
    keeping up with, 57

• *H* •

handicap system
    betting and, 126
    business-related outing, 103
    determination of handicap, 64
    importance of, 65–66
    information on, 66
    overview of, 15, 64
    pro-ams and, 105
Hassan II Trophy, 82, 106
Havemeyer, Theodore A., 15
hazard
    dropping new ball where first
        entered, 133
    moving loose impediments, 19,41
    touching ground in, 30
    water hazard, 44–45
Hewitt, Brian, 113
history
    of golf, 11–13
    of rules, 9–10
hitting
    between ropes on driving range, 81
    fans at tournaments and, 108
    "Fore!," 56

group in front and, 56
    workers, 56
Hog Press, 130
hole, ball overhanging, 40
"holes up," 34
Hong Kong, golf association in, 152
Honourable Company of Edinburgh
        Golfers. *See* Gentlemen Golfers of
        Leith, The
host
    drinking and, 95
    embarrassing, 77
    following lead of, 76
    thanking, 77

• *I* •

Iceland golf association, 152
impediments, moving, 38, 41
Indian Golf Union, 153
indicating line of play, 37
interference by immovable
        obstruction, 43
Internet. *See* Web sites
interpretation of rules
    advice, asking, 50
    movable obstructions, 49
    overview of, 48
    playing out of turn, 49
    scorecard, signing, 50
Irish golf association, 153
Irwin, Hale, 29

• *J* •

Jack Nicklaus Memorial
        Tournament, 112
Jacobsen, Pete, 96
Jamaica Golf Association, 153
James II, 11
Japan Golf Association, 153
Jenkins, Dan, 63
Johnson, Mark, 20
Jones, Bobby, 68, 111
Jones, Steve, 82
junk bets, 129

• K •

keeping pace, 104, 136
Kite, Tom, 28
Korea Golf Association, 153

• L •

lashing out, 62
leaning on putter, 58
learning about person by playing golf
   with, 93
Legend of Baggar Vance, The, 133
lifting ball, 39
line of play, indicating, 37
line of putt, 38–40, 58
lining up putts, 57
liquor
   business-related outing, 103
   host and, 95
   municipal courses, 74
looper. *See* caddie
Lopez, Nancy, 96
lost ball
   helping partner look for, 89
   looking for, 59
   obstruction and, 44
   out of bounds, 45
   water hazard, 44–45

• M •

*M*A*S*H,* 134
magazine Web sites, 147
Malaysian Golf Association, 154
Martin, Casey, 113
Masters Tournament of 1968, 50
match play. *See also* tournament play
   overview of, 34
   practicing and, 36
McCord, Gary, 96
McCormack, Mark, 90, 93
Met Golfer magazine, 3
Metropolitan Golf Association, 69
Mexican Golf Association, 154
Mexico, 13, 22
Moroccan golf association, 154
movement of fans at tournament, 108

moving loose impediments, 41
mulligan, 59
municipal courses
   betting at, 74
   dress code, 74
   liquor, 74
   overview of, 73
   tips for, 74

• N •

Nabisco Championship, 106
Nassau, 127–128
Nelson, Byron, 123
Nelson, Willie, 26, 47
Netherlands Golf Federation, 154
New Zealand Golf Association, 154
news Web sites, 147
North America golf associations,
   149–150
Norwegian Golf Federation, 155

• O •

obstructions
   immovable, 43–44
   movable, 39, 42, 49
Official Rules of Golf, The, 1, 12, 33, 48
Open Championship (British Open), 14
Ouimet, Francis, 68
outings
   business-related, 101–103
   celebrity type, 103
   charity-related, 103–104
outlaw drivers, 17, 21–23, 29
out-of-bounds ball, 45

• P •

pace, keeping, 56–58, 62, 104, 136
Palmer, Arnold, 17, 23, 96, 121
Pedernales course, 47
penalties
   caddy asking advice, 121
   clubs, number of, 121
   hitting ball accidentally, 122
   improper drop, 120
   kicking ball accidentally, 123

penalties *(continued)*
  mental effect of, 119
  overview of, 119
  practicing during round, 122
  stroke play event, 122
  substituting ball, 120
  suspension from club, 123
  waiver of rules, 121
person, learning about by playing golf
    with, 93
Peruvian golf association, 155
PGA Tour, 22
Philippino golf association, 155
Phoenix Open, 113
Phoenix Open of 1999, 49
Pine Valley, 4
Pink Lady, 129
Player, Gary, 96
playing ball as it lay, 10
playing out of turn, 49
playing through, 57
Playing with the Pro, 130
Points, 129
practice facility. *See also* driving range;
    putting green
  betting games for, 85
  overview of, 84
practice swing, 37, 57
practicing
  before or between rounds, 36
  during round, 36, 122
pressing the bet, 127
Price, Nick, 96
private courses
  benefits of, 76
  dress code, 77–78
  joining, 76
  overview of, 75
  tips for, 76–77
pro
  business outings and, 96
  listening to, 59
pro shop
  buying from, 102
  checking in at, 59
pro-am tournaments
  best, 106
  etiquette for, 105
  handicap and, 105

having fun at, 105
  overview of, 104
provisional ball, 46
psyching-out opponent, 63, 64, 65
public courses. *See* municipal courses
punctuality, 61, 103
putting green
  ball lost, 44
  children and, 84
  chipping around, 83
  dragging feet on, 59
  leaning on putter on, 58
  leaving, 58
  limiting number of balls, 83
  line of putt, 38–40, 58
  overview of, 82
  pin and, 83
  relief from immovable
      obstructions, 43
  standing behind person on, 58
  treatment of, 83

• R •

R&A. *See* Royal & Ancient Golf Club of
    St. Andrews
Reagan, Ronald, 81
"Regulations for the Game of Golf," 11
relief from immovable obstruction, 43
repairing putting green, 39
respecting course, 102
Rippey, George, 61, 131
roadies, 130
Robbins, Kelly, 49
round
  building relationship with client
      during, 89
  practicing during, 122
  time limit, 58
Royal & Ancient Golf Club of
    St. Andrews (R&A)
  formation of, 13–14, 17
  overview of, 13
  "Regulations for the Game of Golf," 11
  responsibility of, 14
  rules of, 9
  Rules of Golf Committee, 12–13
  "spring-like effect," 22–23
  USGA and, 12

rule-making, milestones in, 17
rules
  best, 18
  common sense and, 30–31
  devotion to, 28–30
  dumbest, 19–20
  history of, 9–10
  importance of, 16
  interpretation of, 48–50
  most controversial, 21–23
  overview of, 9
  Web sites, 147
Rules of Golf Committee (R&A), 12–13

• *S* •

sandbagger, 66, 126
Sandies, 85
sandy, 129
Sankaty Head, 68
scorecard, signing, 50, 119
Scottish golf associations, 155
searching for ball, 134
Secession golf course, 69
self-policing, 16, 27–28, 31
shaking hands, 61, 64
sharing clubs, 35
shoes
  changing, 77
  soft spikes, 75
  spike holes from, 39
Shoot-out, 85
shopping Web sites, 148
short game area, 84
shorts, wearing, 78
shot preparation, 57
side cheese, 129
Singapore Golf Association, 156
single, playing as, 57
Skins, 128
soft spikes, 75
Solheim Cup of 2000, 49
Sorenstam, Anika, 49
South African Golf Federation, 156
Spanish golf association, 156
spectators. *See* fans
sports, golf compared to, 26–28
sportsmanship, 64
"spring-like effect," 12, 17, 21–23, 29

St. Andrews, Scotland, 11, 13
Stadler, Craig, 20, 30–31
stance, building, 19, 30
standing
  astride or on line of putt, 40
  behind person putting, 58
  to side of player, 59, 62
steel shaft, 17
Stephens, Jack, 95
Strange, Curtis, 31
strangers and betting, 127
stroke
  conceding, 121
  playing while other ball in motion, 40
stroke play
  consideration of opponent, 18
  holing out, 122
  overview of, 34
  practicing and, 36
"stymie rule," 11, 17
surface of putting green, testing, 40
suspension from club, 123
Sutton, Hal, 113
Swedish Golf Federation, 156
swing, commenting on, 89
Swiss golf association, 157

• *T* •

Take Ho, 85
talking
  addressing ball, 56
  attempted psych-out, 63–65
  complaining, 60
  fans at tournaments, 108
  holding up group, 57
  jokes, 95
  running commentary, 62
  swing, commenting on, 89
  verbal abuse, 60
  while someone is swinging, 2, 136
Targets, 85
Taylor, F. Morgan "Buzz," 21
teams, picking, 126
tee
  having honor on, 18
  picking up, 58
teeing ground, 34
telling jokes, 95

testing surface of putting green, 40
Thailand Golf Association, 157
throwing clubs, 59, 62–63
thunderstorms, 134
time limit, 58
Tin Cup, 81, 133, 135
tipping, 71–72
tips
  betting in golf, 126–127
  municipal courses, 74
  offering, 89, 90
  private courses, 76, 77
titanium drivers, 12, 17, 21–23, 29
"to play," 34
Tour Championship of 2000, 110
tournament play. *See also* autographs
  attendance at, 110
  etiquette for, 61–64
  fans and, 107–108, 110–113
  gamesmanship, 65
  outbursts during, 63
  overview of, 60
travel Web sites, 148

• *U* •

United Kingdom, golf association
    in, 157
United States Golf Association (USGA).
    See also handicap system
  Bob Jones Award, 28
  formation of, 12, 15, 17
  overview of, 13
  publication of, 1
  R&A and, 12
  responsibility of, 15
  "spring-like effect," 22–23
unplayable ball, 19, 47
unplayable lie, 135
U.S. Amateur Public Links, 15
U.S. Mid-Amateur, 15
U.S. Open of 1946, 123
USGA. *See* United States Golf
    Association
USGA Museum and Library, 16

• *V* •

Venezuelan golf association, 157
verbal abuse, 60

• *W* •

waiver of rules or penalties, 121
Walker Cup, 15
walking ahead of group, 56
walking course, 91
water hazard, ball lost in, 44–45
weather, 25, 134
Web sites
  associations, 149–151, 153–155, 158
  courses, 148
  news, 147
  rules, 147
  shopping, 148
  travel, 148
Welsh Golfing Union, 158
Western Golf Association's Chick Evans
    Foundation, 68
Whistling Straits, 69
Wigwam Resort, The, 69
William IV, 14
winner, description of, 34
winning, 94
Wolf, 128
Woods, Tiger, 31, 49, 110
World War II, 51

• *Z* •

Zimbabwe Golf Association, 158

Notes

Notes

FOR DUMMIES
BOOK REGISTRATION

Register This Book and Win!

We want to hear from you!

Visit **dummies.com** to register this book and tell us how you liked it!

- ✔ Get entered in our monthly prize giveaway.
- ✔ Give us feedback about this book — tell us what you like best, what you like least, or maybe what you'd like to ask the author and us to change!
- ✔ Let us know any other *For Dummies* topics that interest you.

Your feedback helps us determine what books to publish, tells us what coverage to add as we revise our books, and lets us know whether we're meeting your needs as a *For Dummies* reader. You're our most valuable resource, and what you have to say is important to us!

Not on the Web yet? It's easy to get started with *Dummies 101: The Internet For Windows 98* or *The Internet For Dummies* at local retailers everywhere.

Or let us know what you think by sending us a letter at the following address:

For Dummies Book Registration
Dummies Press
10475 Crosspoint Blvd.
Indianapolis, IN 46256

**BESTSELLING
BOOK SERIES**